LAND OF THE MAYAS
Yesterday and Today

The "malevolent" or "drought" version of the Long-nosed Rain God. Note the exposed bone of the lower jaw; the lashes of the unseen eyes are probably celts or battle-axes. His distended ears are a characteristic of the nobility. The extended tongue in the figure on the ankle is a symbol of fire. The emblems on the god's headdress, the face emerging from his arm, the serpent-belt, and the frog in his hand are symbols of rain.

Carleton Beals

LAND OF THE MAYAS

Yesterday and Today

*illustrated
with photographs by
Marianne Greenwood*

*Abelard-Schuman
London
New York
Toronto*

© Copyright 1966 by Carleton Beals
Library of Congress Catalogue Card Number: AC 66-10561
First published in Great Britain in 1967

LONDON	NEW YORK	TORONTO
Abelard-Schuman Limited	Abelard-Schuman Limited	Abelard-Schuman Canada Limited
8 King St. WC2	6 West 57th St.	896 Queen St. W

Printed in the United States of America

Contents

Photographs

LAND OF THE MAYAS
Yesterday and Today

1 The Memories of the Mayas

The Mayas of today work and play alongside the great carved stone temples and palaces of their ancestors of more than a thousand years ago. The corn in their fields rustles against ancient walls. The bright red coffee berries ripen over the half-buried statues of old gods. The fronds of banana trees cast elongated shadows on the elaborate patterns of the richly-designed stone columns, the *stelae*, of the Quiriguá ruins in Guatemala. The agave plants, which now provide sisal for the harvest machines of the United States, Argentina, and the Soviet Union, form stiff, spiny frames for carved jaguars, snakes, and crocodiles.

At the present time, the Mayas number about two million. They live in the same areas in Mexico, Belice (British Honduras), Guatemala, and Honduras as did their ancestors. For nearly a thousand miles and for more than a thousand years, they built handsome cities and wore beautiful robes of dyed cotton or bird feathers at a time when northern Europeans were still wearing animal skins, living in leaky huts, and eating raw meat.

They were a great people at a time when the Roman Empire
had almost vanished and when Europe was in the Dark Ages.
Europe as we know it did not yet exist.

The old buildings—battered by war and conquest, by storms
and floods—are eaten away by the jungle, smothered by powerful vines, and split apart by the seeds of trees that sprout and
grow into mighty giants. Such ruins are to be found alongside
nearly every village and town, river and lake, all the way from
Chichen Itza, the majestic temple city of Yucatán, to the pyramids of Copán that lie in the arm of a powerful river in Honduras. Owls, the fateful Moan Birds of the Mayas, hoot through
the empty temple halls of Palenque in Chiapas, Mexico, above
silent stone owls that have become blurred from the winds and
waters of eleven hundred years.

Other lost cities lie deep in forests where even the paths
have disappeared. On every hillside, wooden plows turn up
shards of pottery on which once were glazed plumed warriors
of the Eagles and of the Jaguars.

The ancient Mayas—as do the present-day Mayas—built their
houses and planted their corn, beans, hot chilies, and squashes
on the limestone cap of Yucatán, a hot, dry, often treeless world.
They drew water then, as do their modern counterparts, from
the sacred wells, the *cenotes*, where the crust of the earth had
broken through to hidden rivers. From those wells, in modern
times, have been dredged forth heaps of pottery and stone
gods, carved jade and jewels, gold and silver—all objects thrown
into them centuries ago as offerings to the gods.

Here in Yucatán and on adjacent Cozumel Island, a place of
forests, the ancients built splendid cities that still survive, such
as Chichen Itza, Uxmal, Sayil, Tulúm on the coast, and a dozen
others—all cities of stone.

They dwelt, as do their descendants, all through the dense
forests of Quintana Roo, the jungle land of *chicle*, which is the
sap of the sapodilla, or *zapote*, tree and the raw material from

Sugar cane plantation

which chewing gum is made. The word "chicle" is from an Aztec word meaning "gum."

In the forests of Chiapas, Mexico, in the ninth century, they built their finest city of all time, Palenque, overlooking a lordly valley. It was their supreme achievement in architecture, art, and city planning. In the forests of Chiapas, too, stands the city of Bonampak, where the walls are covered with frescoes which are the most notable painting of the New World.

They built similar cities all along the Usumacinta River, the River of Ruins, that loops like a tiger for hundreds of miles from the Guatemalan highlands north to the Gulf of Mexico. On its banks, the skilled builders of the early empire erected the massive structures of the cities of Agua Azul, which means "Blue Water," Yaxchilán, and Piedras Negras, for "Black Stones."

On the Rio Hondo, the "Deep River," that flows from northern Guatemala, too, but out to the lonely palm-studded shores of a forgotten bay in far Belice, they founded many other communities, among them mighty Uaxactún, perhaps the original Mayan settlement from which their culture radiated out to all neighboring points of the compass.

There, in the Petén District, the jungle is as dense and as tall as in Central Africa. Yet, enormous plains also open out for the corn fields, and for the great sugar-cane plantations of later days. (The early Mayas did not know sugar cane.) Originally, the archaeologists claim, this area was densely inhabited. Later, most of the population deserted Yucatán, perhaps because of enemies, drought, or plague; but shortly before the Spaniards came in the early fifteen-hundreds, people moved back to the old Petén centers such as Naranjo and Tikal, among others.

Beyond Petén, farther to the south, stretches more Mayan country, Alta Verapaz, "Upper True Peace," where the soil is rich and deep. Here is lovely Lake Cristóbal, the "Liquid Sky of Dreams." "Within it may be seen," writes a Guatemalan poet, "everything, the sun, the moon, the stars, the mountains."

Ruins of Tikal, one of the first Mayan cities, built centuries before Christ

Mayas from the region of Alta Verapaz, Guatemala

On its shores stands a town of the same name, originally founded and named by the Mayas Cacchoc Chichó for "Brave Lion." It is still famous for its fine pottery.

Even farther to the south are the provinces of Baja Altapaz and the magic land of Tezulutlán, full of rivers, lakes, marshes, rugged mountains, and deep valleys. It has a number of picturesque towns such as Salamá, set in a wide, fertile plain. Salamá was founded before the coming of the Spaniards by Aztec invaders. Old cypress trees, the giants of the forest, tower about its church. In a nearby park, underneath a sacred giant ceiba, the wild cotton tree, peasants spread out their wares —cacao beans and fruits, woven blankets, pottery and etched gourds—as their forebears must have done in the days of Christ. A hundred years ago, a French naturalist who lived there said it had no doctor because "The people here are all so healthy, a doctor could not make a living."

Under high mountains bearing Mayan names, lies Rabinal, where citrus orchards yield oranges "sweeter and more delicious than a bowl of sugar-cane syrup." Not far away is San Chomo, where the Mayas made, and still make, a strong liquor called *agua*—this is the national firewater. Nearby are the ruins of Pueblo Viejo, the "Old Town."

The chief center, as it probably was for the first Mayas, is Cobán, a pretty little town set among hills and rushing little streams in deep, dense valleys. It is hot, damp country, where —the saying goes—it rains "thirteen months" a year; these rains are heavy deluges. Everything is constantly bursting into new green, even the fence posts. Green climbers spread over the rust-red tiled roofs. New gourd and chayote vines creep across tiled entrances and turn to penetrate doors and windows. All the little streams and the Cobán River are full of fish. New trees sprout and shoot up as high as twenty feet in a week. Others may take years to grow even half that height. All the houses are shaded by magnolia, acacia, ceiba, and palm trees. Flowers grow all year in great masses of color.

The Mayan kingdom spread out. To the east, the Mayan

Lake Atitlán

peoples claimed part of northern Honduras and there built their far-flung city of Copán, one of the most memorable archaeological sites of the Americas.

They surged up over the mountains, learning to live in the cold country against the sky, and built their houses by the lovely lakes of Amatitlán and Atitlán and around the slim snow-capped volcanoes.

One is tempted to call it the most beautiful country on earth. There are only two seasons, the wet and the dry, for it has an all-year-round spring climate. The air is balmy and sweet. There is no smog. Such was the empire of the Quiché-Mayas, and such is their empire today.

Lake Atitlán: Was the first dawn like this?

Its founders left behind records in clay and in stone. In hieroglyphics, they inscribed the dates of their history and of their
buildings onto statues and pottery and in painted books, or
codices. The Yucatán books of *Chilám Balám* give the historical
record from A.D. 176, which is usually called the beginning of
the "historical period," up to the Spanish Conquest.

Their codices were painted on paper made from the bark of
the fig tree, on parchment, and on leather. Those on paper or
parchment were folded like books and provided with very thin
covers of board. The early Church authorities destroyed as
many of them as they could—a sad loss for man's historians;
their picture-writing and parchment scrolls documented the
history, medicine, fiestas, and religion of the inscribers. Only
three are now left in the entire world. The *Popol Vuh*, "the
Book of the Quiché," has been translated into Spanish. It tells
of the creation of earth, the animals, the birds, the sun, the
moon and the stars, and of mankind, as well as the stories of
their gods, their rulers, and their wars.

The Mayan wise men were great astronomers and knew the
precise movements of the celestial bodies at a time when
Europeans still believed that the world was flat and that the
sun revolved around the earth. They worked out a calendar
even more accurate than the one we use today in the Western
World. They were remarkable mathematicians, too. They discovered the concept of zero a thousand years before the scholars of Europe did.

According to old Mayan calendar records, the Quiché-Maya
era began November 10, 3485 B.C. The first actual recorded
stone date is 96 B.C., deciphered from glyphs on the Tuxtla
statue from San Andrés Tuxtla. The next recorded date, on a
Museum of Leyden plate, is A.D. 61. The earliest recorded date
at Tikal is A.D. 216 although the city was founded apparently
fifteen hundred years before this.

Thus, long before the time of Christ, the Quiché-Maya began
building their great stone cities in the jungles of northern Guatemala. Some of these cities were finally uncovered by the

New cities built on top of earlier sets of pyramids, Tikal

archaeologists, but there are scores more that have never been excavated or studied and are known only to the Mayas who now live and work there. The ones told about by the scholars are mostly newer cities, built on top of older cities. Some new cities, such as Copán in Honduras, were erected on top of at least two earlier sets of pyramids; they were built larger and higher than the old ones.

Two of the oldest settlements known—perhaps the oldest of all—are Uaxactún and Tikal in northern Petén. The great eras of

Mayan culture after Christ may have radiated out from those two mighty areas — north to Yucatán, south to Copán and beyond, east into Belice (where they built the great city of Lubaantún and many more), then east to the lakes and the Salvadorean border.

Uaxactún, "Eight Stones," gives us the early date A.D. 61, but the city must have been older than that. When it was more or less abandoned in 638, it had a population of 50,000. Uaxactún was resettled when the Mayas fled south from Yucatán shortly before the Spaniards came.

Like all early Quiché-Maya cities, Uaxactún was built around a central plaza with pyramid, temples, government buildings, palaces, and handsome homes for rulers and priests. A wide staircase, decorated with carvings and statues, led to the temple atop the pyramid. There were ample courts for games and ceremonies. A favorite Mayan game resembled modern basketball. It was played with a hard rubber ball. As in soccer, the ball could only be thrown back by using the elbow, fist or hip, without using the hands or feet. It had to be passed through a stone ring, often ornately carved and studded with gems, that projected vertically from the stone walls.

Tikal, not very distant, became an even greater city. Certainly its thirty-foot-thick walls and the wide and steeply sloping staircases that give access to its lofty temples indicate that it was one of the first cities ever built by the Mayas; it is said to have been started about fourteen hundred years before Christ. That was in the time of the Pharaohs, nearly a thousand years before the greatness that was Greece. The Romans were living in a tiny primitive village on the banks of the Tiber. According to some authorities, Tikal came to have as many as two million people. If so, it was larger than the capital city of the Aztecs, Tenochtitlán, where Mexico City now stands, and remained the largest city in the Americas for some time.

One building was the tallest in the New World for many, many centuries; constructed on three planes, it was five stories high. The upper three stories rested one above the other to

Mayan ruins, Tikal

form a square tower. Into the stones, statues, and numerous *stelae* are carved the figures of plumed serpents and warriors and gods who wear ornate headdresses of feathered serpents, jaguars, and pumas. The feathered serpent was the emblem of Kukulcan, the god of life. Many sets of great, staring stone eyes look out upon all eternity. Turtles, crocodiles, snails, birds, and flowers are elaborately depicted, and numerous glyphs tell of time and its great events.

In Tikal, the Mayas built what must have been the highest straight flight of stairs in the world; it rose steeply to a temple. Its soaring height may have represented a desire to rise above the humdrum toil of their lives, to free their souls from their bodies, and to get closer to the heavens. Their poetry, their art, their records, their knowledge of astronomy show this eternal urge to reach the sky, the sun, the moon, the stars, and to be part of the great universe. Had they been able to, they most certainly would have initiated space-travel.

When the Spaniards began closing in, in an effort to resist the invader, the people of Tikal erected their last temple-fortress on an island in nearby Lake Petén. The conquistadors were killing their people and defiling their gods by tearing down their temples, smashing their idols, and setting their sacred scrolls afire.

But another city, Copán in Honduras, was long undiscovered by the invaders. To get to ancient Copán formerly required five days on muleback; now there is a small airport. This magnificent city was first mapped in 1839 by an American, John Lloyd Stephens, the famous early Central American explorer. But just when the first temple-pyramid was built here, no one has ventured to guess. In successive eras, new and larger temples were built on top of the old ones. The space between was filled with rubble. The main pyramid faces the big central plaza and rises about 130 feet. A steep, carved stairway gives access to the uppermost temples.

A vast quadrangle with a number of similar plazas is surrounded by walls thirty to seventy feet high. These walls are faced inside by stone steps, thus making the entire area an enormous stadium. Some seventy structures within and outside the walls are crowded into an area measuring less than half a square mile. Nearly all the constructions are built of a soft green stone. Some are half-hidden in jungle growth.

The temple atop the main pyramid has two rooms: an inner one, dark and narrow—the true sanctuary—and an outer room, almost like a portico. The size of rooms was limited by the fact that the Mayas never learned to make a true arch. They merely jutted each stone slightly beyond the other until the two sides finally met. A huge capstone was put on top. Thus, the doorways here—as in the structures built centuries later at Palenque, Chichen Itza, and Uxmal—form inverted V's, often of almost majestic height.

Ruins of Copán, Honduras

The famous Copán Hieroglyphic Stairway is in the east court. Here, too, stands a most ornate temple. Its entrance is guarded by enormous figures that rear up from a base of skulls. Serpent tails meet at the top of the archway. The drum-shaped altars have little decoration. They are, however, solidly carved with glyphs, some two-tailed dragons, turtles, and jaguars.

Wall sculptures adorn nearly all the entrances. The faces, with plumes and huge handlelike ears, ancient symbol of nobility, bear such dates as A.D. 383, 447, 502, and 523. They appear strong, but nevertheless placid. One—apparently a god, perhaps the god of fire or of the sun—is depicted with enormous opaque

Detail from an ancient glyph

eyes and its tongue projecting from between its heavy lips.
Some of the heads are shown in the mouths of enormous loop-
ing snakes. One altar holds a jaguar god with a great rounded
head, down-slanting slit eyes, and enormous teeth. He sits with
one foreleg before him at a right angle. There are many carved
and inscribed stones about, from six to thirty feet high. Some
such *stelae* have full-length figures and are wider at the top.
Nearly all are flanked by calendar hieroglyphics. But some have
just glyphs set in regular rectangles; each such glyph has a head
of the god of the day and figures indicating the date.

Lubaantún in Belice is another mighty Mayan city. It lies

between two creeks that sometimes become great torrents. A
series of terraces form a hatchet-shaped area of seven-and-a-
half acres. Seventy edifices—great temples, palaces, funeral
monuments, and corn granaries—comprise the center. The main
amphitheater covers nearly a third of an acre; it is paved with
cement or cut stone. The buildings are so arranged — for example, one pyramid is elevated behind another — that people
can view whatever ceremonies or games are going on, no
matter where they are situated. The entire area served as a
vast coliseum, or stadium, for at least ten thousand people.
Lubaantún was a combination fortress, theater, religious and
governmental center—and a snow-white island, fifty feet high.

(Several other great stone centers are not far distant. And in
the same zone, there are dozens of others that have not been
studied.)

The figurines, sculptures, and other art here span a period of
a thousand years from the primitive work of Copán through
more elaborate art like that of Palenque and Chichen Itza. One
goddess is depicted kneeling at an altar, and holding in one
hand a basket of fruit and cakes, and in the other, a man's head.
Many of the female figures wear the costume of the modern
Maya and elaborate necklaces and earrings. The headdresses
are also similar to those worn today.

The two most accessible ruins in Yucatán are Chichen Itza
and Uxmal. Both represent high peaks in Mayan architecture.
The "Governor's House" at Uxmal with its façade of inlaid stone
carving, the great façade at Hochob, and the carved mosaics
of Palenque are superb examples of this.

Perhaps the greatest Mayan achievement of all, so far as we
know, is Palenque in Chiapas. This lies on a 2,000-foot-high
mountain shelf situated at the edge of a precipice from which
cataracts tumble down from half a dozen streams running from
four valleys. One of these valleys—up to where a stream edges
through tight canyon walls—is wholly occupied by Palenque.
Below is a great expanse of plain, jungle, and lesser mountains.
None of the sites of the old cities was better chosen for defense,

or for scenic beauty. At Palenque, there breathes the spirit of a people who have reached the pinnacle of achievement, art, and leisure.

The chief palace of the compact group of buildings is almost a city in itself. It rises from a terrace faced with stone. Its vaulted galleries face four great inner courts. These are entered by way of doorways separated by huge square pillars. Everywhere, the panels are of stucco with pressed or molded designs instead of the customary stone carvings; the colors are faded by now. The edifice is topped by a tall square tower, four stories high, with an interior staircase that is guarded today by hornet nests. All the structures are graceful rather than massive; the old sturdy, primitive solidity has given way to poised assurance.

The massive buildings and carvings of Copán, Tikal, and other more southern cities have the impact of primitive strength; of kinship with storms, earthquakes, and all the forces that periodically shake the world. Palenque is more serene, more mature, and more beautiful. Copán has been compared to the Gothic Period, and Palenque, to the Versailles Period. Craftsmanship, instead of being primarily a ritual for the gods and an expression of man's early striving, has become an end in itself.

Such are some of the glories of the Mayas whose empire was over-run by the Spaniards despite their resistance for a hundred years. History passed the old cities by. But the Mayan people lived on, deep in their jungle shelters, deep in the ravines, and deep in the mountains. They still live in their old empire. They know that their power is gone and that they are a subjugated people. But the old culture—the love of art, of music, of flowers, of animals—lives on. They are the Mayas of yesterday as well as of today.

In the busy markets, many of the faces of today look just like some of those that were, ages ago, carved into stone, molded into pottery, or painted in pre-Spanish picture scrolls or codices. And in the pottery used today, little changed in

Before the market opens

People of Lake Atitlán

By the old pyramid

shape, one can see the same designs and the same animals, flowers, and warriors of the past. The old days are also relived in delicate white traceries on the black gourds which serve as receptacles, and on terra-cotta piggy banks. They are unfolded in even the patterns of woven fabrics.

Like the people in the temple carvings, those in the market often have round faces with rather flat noses and full lips. But some are more reminiscent of the stone reliefs on the palace walls in that they have long, powerful noses that seem to extend in a straight line from sloping foreheads. Some Mayan noses are curved like parrot beaks, and still others are almost as thin as knife-blades, the cheeks hollowed alongside them. Their large black eyes may seem fierce and fiery at first glance, but are actually liquid and gentle. How quickly those earnest, stern faces break into smiles at the first friendly word!

The long lineage of the people is revealed by more than face and form. The hairdos of the modern Mayan women, the smooth sweep of hair into two coiled disks at the back, are matched in the old temple stones as are the striped head coverings which drape squarely in the front and fall above the neck at the back for protection from the strong sun.

In the upland cold country, 10,000 feet above the sea, however weak the sun, the violet rays are powerful. There the headdress, often almost like a wig, is a serpentlike mass of woollen coils and knots. The women wear the same sort of sleeveless blouses, the rainbow-colored *huipil* cut square and low on the chest, the same bright sashes, and the same long skirts embroidered with flowers and animals, moons and stars. About their necks are the customary necklaces of jade, of red and black seeds, and of snakelike filigreed silver. Those amazingly flexible silver cords are also looped into a circle and cast over bride and groom in the wedding ceremony as a symbol of everlasting union. Or, they are worn as girdles. One can easily be worn as a choker of many strands about the neck.

Three thousand years are behind the Mayas of today. In many places, the old world has crumbled away. The white

Woman and child of the cold country

Man of the highlands

stones of Chakantín are scattered over a wide area beyond the present shabby town of La Libertad. The palace stones of the old fortress on the island in Lake Petén have mostly vanished, and the present village of Flores with its fisherfolk is so crowded with thatched houses that one often has to walk through them in lieu of streets. Their inhabitants smile, seemingly undisturbed by the intrusion.

Few peoples on earth today seem closer to Nature than do the Mayas; they seem to be almost a part of Nature. Most of them are ignorant of the glories of the past. They live on within the confines of the old empire, poor and often abused, but mostly busy and happy with their lot. There is little evidence that what we know as civilization would benefit them greatly, and it is unlikely that it could increase their love for beauty, music, dancing. The few so-called civilized towns are mostly miserable spots. The real Mayan world is still the jungle and they are children of the jungle. Their corn fields, their simple houses, their families, their animals and birds and flowers are enough.

They were, and still are, a proud people. The Mayas of Yucatán resent being called Mexicans. Actually, in days of crisis, they were as loyal to Mexico as those of the interior. They resent the Guatemalan *Ladinos*, the men of mixed blood who come into their villages and round them up at gunpoint to work on the coffee plantations for a few *centavos* a day or to serve in the Army, and who collect taxes for the far-off government of Guatemala City, for them still the center of the Spanish Conquest.

The Mayas have always been an independent, self-sufficient

Conchita,
Sisal,
Yucatán

people. They still grow and process their food, make their utensils, sew their clothes, and build their houses in their own way. They cherish their arts and live by the precepts of their songs and poetry. They train their children to be industrious, loyal, and courageous. They have many virtues and so many joys which people who call themselves civilized have lost in their harsh struggle upward to wealth and power.

They are chiefly a corn-eating people. They grow corn of many shapes and colors—white, yellow and brown, green, red and black—and grind it on hand-carved stones. The first man — and they say he was a Maya — "was made from a kernel of corn."

2 How They Live

"Indian, you travel all the roads of America,
Sometimes over peaks that rise from the earth
And break through the blue curve of heaven to peer at infinity,
Sometimes through the lands that burn
You with the fire of the tropics;
Your feet mount the roads of weariness
You water the distances
With the sweat of your brown muscles;
You still carry on your dark backs
The *cacaxtle*, the crate, of burdens
Laid upon you by Pedro de Alvarado, the Conquistador.

Listen to me;
I, too, am Indian,
Another man of your race,
Another son of America
Who travels along the roads of my life,
Roads sometimes steep, harsh and difficult,
Sometimes level, but rough and wearisome,

And I anoint my road with rebellion,
Sweating I hold tight infinite anxieties,
And I carry my load of anguish
Of hopes and dreams
On the numbed back of my soul.

Indian, let us trade our burdens,
Perhaps your crate of roasting stones,
Of big jars and fruits,
You carry on your back
Is not so heavy
As the enormous load I carry on my soul."

Manuel Chavarría Flores

Everywhere on the mountain trails or the jungle paths, one meets the burden-bearers. In Mexico, one finds loaded burros and mules; there the muleteer is a very picturesque man famed in story and in song. But in Guatemala, though mules are often used, it is man himself who carries the loads to far places. Half bent over, the *cargador,* or burden-bearer, carries heavy bales of coffee and of brown sugar or slatted *cacaxtles,* or crates, held together with rawhide. He carries pottery, fruit, turkeys, and chickens, or nets holding potatoes and gourds. Across his forehead, he wears a woven or rawhide band from which is suspended a tump line to hold the load in place and ease its weight on the bearer's back. The Mayan *cargador* never walks, but goes at a swinging trot that eats up the miles. So used are they to travelling with loads, it has been said that some, after delivering their wares, will load their empty crates or bags with roadside stones so as to keep the same rhythm as they trot home.

Usually, they will stop to talk although they will rarely lay down their burdens. They stand, still half bent, panting slightly, their sweat running into their eyes. They are pleased by the offer of a cigarette, which they accept with a special gesture

Good harvest idol

of thanks. The lighting of it, too, is almost a salutation. They
are friendly, courteous, with open bronze faces and shy smiles.

"Where are you going, my friend?"

"To the market in Chichicastenango."

"That is a long way." (Twenty-two miles.)

"Oh, no, Señor, it is just over the hill, only a step away.
I'm almost there."

"Will you sell me that nice blue jar?"

His eyes drop, his right toe digs into the ground. "Pues no,
Señor, I'm sorry."

"But I will pay you whatever you ask for it."

He shakes his head again. "I sell only in the market, Señor."

"But why is that?"

He finds it difficult to explain. He does not sell just to make
a few *quetzales,* as the Guatemalan *pesos* are called. This is
a minor consideration—the making of money. Sitting in the

market with fellow vendors is almost like going to church. It is a chance to meet friends and strangers, to greet customers and to enjoy the pleasures of bargaining with them, to share his *tortillas* at mealtime. He gathers gossip from distant villages and learns what is happening in the world. It is a ritual that satisfies his soul and his reward for the lonely work in the fields or at the pottery kilns.

Another *cargador* goes by with a big bag of seed corn to be blessed by the village priest before he carries it home for planting. Quite likely, he will at the same time bury an old stone idol alongside the field as a guarantee of a good crop. In

Small marimba *and masked dancer*

some places, there are people who rent out idols for such purposes.

It is not unusual to see from one to four men carrying a heavy *marimba* over the trails. The *marimba,* a kind of xylophone, is a large, three-legged instrument with flat metal strips, or bars, and keys made of a sonorous wood that gives off different tones when struck by sticks with padded rawhide ends. Underneath it hang various-sized gourds to provide resonance. As many as four musicians can play the *marimba* simultaneously.

They go from fiesta to fiesta and play at weddings and christenings, receiving tips and donations, and food and drink, from the villagers. In the mountains, they are likely to wear dark woolen jackets, knee-length pants, little wool caps or felt hats, and nearly always, a dark brown, coarsely-woven *sarape,* or blanket. Their outfit includes, too, a bright red sash. In the cities, where they play in parks and on street corners, in hotel patios and at open-air restaurants, they are usually dressed in white cotton or linen, but they still wear the red sashes.

On the trail, they readily set down their instrument to talk. Sometimes they will play the lively music of their people, which often imitates the songs of their local thrush. The range of the *cenzontle* spans a full major scale.

The wheel is almost unknown in Mayan country. Not even the potter's wheel is in use. The wheel is never seen on the trails and paths. There are some carts in the villages and some cars in the cities. But there is one foreign device that has penetrated even the jungle, the sewing machine. The poorest peasant somehow manages to make time payments on a sewing machine. But for all its whirling wheels, the sewing machine got to the buyer on the back of a *cargador.* So did the brass bed, a much beloved object even in many humble homes. Sometimes it has been sent back by a son who has ventured out into the world. The story is told that one mountain couple preferred to sleep on the customary mat with the bed overhead making a sort of gilded royal canopy.

Not all the cargadores *are men*

Coast plantation workers

Just as modern truckdrivers have their favorite meeting places on the highway for coffee and hamburgers, so the Mayan *cargadores* gather at sundown, perhaps on some high riverbank. They ease their tump lines off their brows and lower their loads. They squat—the Mayan rarely sits—in a circle about a campfire. They toast their *tortillas*, their *tasajo*, or jerked beef, and warm their *atole*, or corn gruel. They talk to each other in a low murmur of Mayan words. They tell tales, sometimes sing songs. Before dawn, they are on the road again.

Walk the long white road to Totuta in Yucatán between the agave fields that stretch far and wide. The agave plant is like a huge artichoke with wide, open, spiny leaves. These are the leaves that provide the fibers for *henequén,* or sisal. Piles of these leaves are heaped beside the house walls to dry before they are sliced up.

Along the level white road, already twinkling with fireflies, the twilight breeze whispers faintly in the *jaracanda* trees that shed red blossoms like drops of blood.

In the town, the oval white-calcimined houses stand close together. The thatched roofs are steep, almost conical. Even the hotel looks the same. Its clean white walls are decorated by a few calendars, a harem scene with gauze-draped beauties and black eunuchs, and several pictures of Christ and of Mary and the Child. The room is provided with a hammock, not a bed; hammocks are cool and also remain free of crawling insects. The room has wooden pegs for clothes, a small table, several rickety cane-bottomed chairs, a metal stand holding a wash-basin and a pitcher, both of heavy porcelain with bright red rose designs. The Mayas are very clean and usually bathe three times a day.

On arrival, one is at once served small terra-cotta cups of either *atole,* ground corn gruel with milk or water, or thick chocolate. Both drinks are always flavored with cinnamon.

Morning is hot and glaring. People stay close to the shadows of the walls. They move and speak softly, but their walk is proud and erect, especially that of the women, for they are accustomed to carrying burdens on their heads. They sleek back their hair from their slanted foreheads and bind it in the two traditional rolls back of their ears. Their one-piece dress, a kind of smock that leaves their arms bare, is embroidered richly in reds, and a golden pattern of orchids and roses, deer, and herons. It reaches to the knees. Below it is worn a full petticoat of delicate lace that rustles over slim brown ankles.

It is the same attire their female ancestors wore a thousand years ago.

The workers go to the fields before daybreak, arriving as the light creeps over the jungle to the east and south to make great walls of black-green. Their sharp, curved machetes slice off the long, fleshy leaves. These are put into piles, bound together, and carried off to the various houses where they will be left to dry before being shredded. The yellowed fibers are treated in liquid vats and bleached almost white. After being dried, the fibers are braided together to make the strong binding twine used in harvest machines, or they are packed in 100- or 200-pound bales to be sent abroad for processing.

Villagers, Hunuciná, Yucatán

Coffee pickers

More and more often, this work is being done by machinery. Toothed machines shred the leaves, braid the fiber, roll it into large balls or onto wooden wheels with end-slats that keep them from rolling.

The local people also make much use of *henequén*. With it, they weave mats, and make bags, nets, and fish nets. Most of these products are dyed bright colors, and often carry designs of fruits, flowers, and animals.

The Mayas are among the most skillful coffee-growers in the world, although few of them own the plantations or even the small coffee farms they work. The largest plantation may contain nearly three thousand acres, but because of the large number of workers required, the conventional size is from fifty to a hundred acres. Some Mayas are *colonos*, or share-croppers. Others are housed on the *finca*, or land, and given food rations; hired by the month, they are called *meseros,* the Spanish word for journeymen who are given monthly wages. Others are merely seasonal day laborers.

The coffee lands lie from three to five thousand feet up, above the level of the cattle, banana, and sugar-cane regions but below the temperate-zone level reserved for vegetable crops.

The coffee orchards wreathe the mountainsides like a great white veil when the plants are in flower. Later, as the bean ripens, the hills will seem to be covered with a tapestry of red and green.

It is claimed that Guatemala's best coffee is grown in the Mayan hill country, where the natives will insist that theirs is the *world's* best coffee. Since Guatemalan coffee is considered one of the best grown anywhere, the coffee grown by the Mayas is very fine, indeed.

Skilled workmanship is important. The coffee is a curious plant in that it has to be pampered, for all its sturdiness. The delicate seedlings must be tenderly nursed at exactly the right temperature. As soon as they put out two butterfly leaves, they are set out under shade trees for two years before being transplanted to the permanent *cafetales,* or coffee orchards. Coffee must be grown in shade, although a year-round hot climate is required. The large trees used for shading must have roots that go deep enough not to sap the surface soil. Various kinds of trees, most of them unknown in the more temperate lands, are used; the choice depends on the climate, rainfall, or altitude. In some places, the huge *guayacán,* or guaiacum tree, which is considered a very holy tree, is preferred. Close to the coast, banana trees are often used until the customary larger trees grow to the proper size.

The coffee shrub can be harvested commercially after three years, but it is considered better to wait five years if a large crop is to be obtained year after year. Maximum yield is at about fifteen years. A period of thirty years is the normal productive life span, although good crops have been obtained over as many as sixty years.

A little worker

Coffee pickers

The fields must be weeded three times a year, and the plants must be properly pruned. Usually, they are not allowed to grow higher than a man, a precaution which simplifies picking and guarantees a heavier yield.

Picking has to be done by trained fingers lest the berries and the shrub be injured. The berries lie in clusters at the base of large, shiny leaves, but each berry must be picked separately. The children soon learn how to do this and are put to work at an early age. Women are more adept at it than are most men. No machines can do it. This means that coffee will never become a cheap product, for, everywhere, the workers are demanding and gradually getting better pay. The average family can pick about half an acre a day, but it takes many nimble fingers to gather the 125,000,000 pounds or so that Guatemala exports each year.

The red berry has a twin green seed buried in its firm flesh. The red hull and the flesh have to be stripped away. Here and there, this is now being done by simple machines, although the old-style barefoot treading is still not uncommon.

The beans are allowed to ferment before they are washed. But the seed still retains a jelly, so they must be spread out in the sun to dry. They are stirred constantly with large wooden rakes. Today, there are also mechanized driers. Since the cleaned twin seeds are divided by a thin parchment, or membrane, they again have to be separated and cleaned by winnowing.

Still, the processing is not complete for the seeds are encased in a delicate silver-colored skin, which is removed by machinery. The final product, a blue-green bean, is slightly transparent, smooth, and a bit spongy. The bean will retain its flavor almost indefinitely.

The picking season, from October to mid-January, is a colorful time. The bright clothes of the workers move among the coffee shrubs in the shade of the great trees. Occasionally, the workers will sing as they drop the berries into their baskets. Various coffee fiestas are celebrated with music and dance before and after the season. Ceremonies to placate the old gods are solemnly conducted; often the priest will bless the crop before the work begins and when it is over, too.

There is always a pungent aroma in the air, as some of the coffee is roasted on the spot. The Guatemalans roast it with brown sugar and char the bean to retain the flavor longer and to sharpen it. The best coffee is made by grinding it immediately after roasting.

In Guatemala, the beverage is usually made with coffee essence, which is kept in glass decanters and poured as needed into a cup of boiling-hot water. The coffee is so concentrated that only about one teaspoon of essence need be used. The brew is liked by Guatemalans, but by few Americans, or people in other countries. Much of the aroma and taste are lost in the making of the essence.

> "This is my song of the coffee berry
> Red as the lips of a pretty girl.
> Sweet is the smell of coffee,
> Nimble are the fingers of the coffee-picker,
> Lively are the feet that dance
> Around the coffee bush. Sing.
> The song of the coffee berry."

3   Chicleros and Weavers

The Mayas who gather *chicle*, or chewing gum, in the jungles of Quintana Roo, Petén, and Belice are mostly a wild and sturdy breed. They go into the deep forests loaded with their climbing ropes, sharply curved machetes, and receptacles for catching and boiling the sap of the *zapote chico*. The words "little sapodilla," do not refer to the size of the tree, which is a majestic giant, but rather to the size of the fruit as compared to that of another variety, the *zapote grande*, or "big sapodilla."

The round *zapote chico* is about the size of a baseball, while the *zapote grande* is oblong in shape and about three times as large. Both have thin, hard, brown shells covered with shaggy reddish fibers. The brick-red flesh inside is soft and pastelike. It covers a large, shiny-black seed. In the larger fruit, the seed is long and tapering. Both fruits are delicious, although the smaller one is tastier and sweeter.

The sapodilla's foliage is evergreen and its leaves are large, broad, and shiny. Its reddish wood is hard and durable. The *chicle* comes from the latex, or sap, of the tree, which runs out copiously in the early spring.

Chicle *country: the great rain forest*

Chicle was introduced into the United States, it is said, by Antonio López de Santa Ana, the Mexican dictator, who fought Sam Houston over Texas. While in exile in New York City, he was visited by a young newspaper man named Adams, and during the interview, Santa Ana drew a chunk of grey substance from his pocket, bit off a piece, and chewed. Santa Ana let Adams try it, and Adams was amazed that the gumlike substance could not be chewed up, but retained the same even consistency. He founded the Adams Chewing Gum Company. This happened about the time of the Mexican War in 1836.

To supply the American craving for chewing gum, an enormous industry was begun deep in the jungles of Central America and Mexico. The *chicleros*, or chicle-gatherers, threaded the jungles looking for *zapote* trees to tap. A *chiclero* would find one big tree. (He was lucky if he found more within a radius of a mile or so.) He would unburden himself of his load, cast his rope around one of the branches high above the ground, kick off his sandals, and pull himself up by toeing the bark. With his machete, he would make a connected series of zigzag slits all down the trunk. The sap would flow down and drip into a receptacle pegged in slightly above the ground. This he would empty into a vat to be boiled down.

Once the sap is the right consistency, it is allowed to cool into a solid grey mass, which is then bound up in cloth or rawhide with liana cords. It is ready to be carried to the collecting center, which may be anywhere from a day to a week or more away. There it is weighed, and he is paid off; any advances previously made to outfit him are deducted. Most *chicle* formerly was exported through the British Honduras, where the traffic was monopolized by an enterprising Belician. The chewing-gum companies dealt only with him. He was many times a millionaire.

The *chiclero* must endure many hardships. He has to be an expert woodsman in order to orient his travel. Often he must face tropical storms, occasionally of cyclonic intensity. The heavy rains keep him soaked to the skin. In most of this region,

The jungle by the Caribbean

the rainfall is over four hundred inches a year, and he must be able to ford swollen rivers and to avoid treacherous marshes.

On occasion, he must flee for his life from the onslaught of armies of ants who follow their own tracks that run like white scars through the jungle. If he suffers an injury, he rubs it with the earth of the forest, which contains fungi with great healing power. Often he walks barefoot for it protects him from the infection of insect bites. But he then runs another danger, that of getting borers under his toenails and then developing dreadful ulcers. Some insects may lay larvae in his hip and the ensuing cavity will be as big as his fist. But these are rare mishaps, and the painful sores soon heal up.

Malaria is all too common and often fatal. The most dreaded disease is yaws, a skin infection causing enormous tumors that burrow into the flesh, particularly that of the face where they sometimes eat away the nose. While there are those who believe it is a contagious disease, recent theories link it to dietary deficiency. In any event, it is now quickly cured inexpensively by a small amount of penicillin.

There is the threat of poisonous plants and snakes, some of which are deadly. But this is not as common a hazard as is usually believed. Actually, there are many more snakes in temperate and northern climes, and a *chiclero* can travel in the jungle for weeks on end without seeing even one. Nor is there much danger from wild animals which, unless provoked, avoid man. The peccary, or wild pig or boar, is probably his most fearsome adversary. Many *chicleros* carry revolvers, rifles, or

Rio Salado by the Caribbean Sea in the hot country

Puma of Yucatán

shotguns, for such animals provide additional food to add to the usual diet of *pinole*, or parched corn, and *tasajo*, or jerked beef. Small monkeys, jaguars, wolves, pumas, deer, foxes, anteaters, armadillos, porcupines, sloths, enormous lizards, and crocodiles are also about.

It is a beautiful world. Enormous flocks of parrots and macaws wing by, crying raucously. Other brightly feathered birds dart through the dusky shade. The great king buzzard, seldom seen, wheels high overhead. Quintana Roo and the Petén have more kinds of birds than the entire eastern United States, and many North American birds pass through on their way south for the winter.

Giant white, blue, and brown butterflies flutter across and along the trail. Masses of flowers are draped over the trees, and sometimes, the *chiclero* walks under a sky of orchids.

The *chiclero's* greatest enemy is man. Many outlaws, true desperados, have escaped into the jungles. The law does not reach into this area very frequently, and the murderer and criminal often find lasting sanctuary there. Each *chiclero* must be ready to protect himself and the fruit of his work. Sometimes his bundle of *chicle* is highjacked. In the frowzy small towns fringing the jungle, robbers, gamblers, and women entertainers are eager to take away his earnings—to perhaps even murder him for his money. After a long gruelling period of loneliness in the jungle, he is in the mood for human companionship and pleasure of almost any sort.

Highland village

Laborer

Yet, there is no freer man on earth than the bold Mayan *chiclero*. He pays for that freedom by risking not only his health but his life, and enduring the hardships of gathering the *chicle* from the tall *zapote* tree. Freedom, it seems, always has to be earned.

In Cunín, a poor village in Guatemala's mountain sheep country, the chief weaver is Don Antonio. He lives in a three-room adobe house with a steep thatched roof, held up by numerous exposed rafters that also serve as roosts for chickens. His foot-treadle loom stands outdoors under a *ramada*, or shed, where razorback pigs and half-starving dogs come and go.

He is clad in short woollen trousers held up by a red sash. His shanks are bare. He wears a woollen shirt of variegated hues. In cold weather, he dons a light blanket, with a hole in it for his head, and drapes it well over his shoulders on either side. When he cannot go barefoot, he pulls on crude leather sandals.

*Boy of
the cold
country*

His wife María, round and bright-eyed, is dressed in a wrap-around woollen skirt. The top folds are cleverly tucked in at her waist, and make a sort of pouch in the back. She never wears sandals.

She and their two small daughters card the wool, using a sort of currycomb with hardwood teeth, and then spin it on a distaff. He and their boys do the weaving. He dyes wool yarn, which must be bound together very tightly when it is dipped so that the colors will range from white to dark brown or blue and all the shades in between. He is clever at blending the many colors into pleasing designs. He is a speedy worker, and the boys bob up and down eagerly changing the heddle.

María also does the buying and selling and handles the

finances of the household. She is the one who sits in the market in the shade of her tripod of cloth.

"I will buy the whole bolt, Niñita. How much is it?"

"Twenty-five *quetzales*, Señor."

He throws up his hands. "Ah, that is too much. That is an absurd price. I will give you eighteen."

"Señor, you are trying to rob me. But I will give you a bargain today, for I have much to do. Twenty-three *pesos*, Señor, and I am losing money at that miserable price."

Antonio has edged over to listen, but he takes no part in the bargaining. It goes on for a long time. The buyer finally offers her twenty *quetzales*. She shakes her head, and he turns away.

Young mother at the market

"Señor, I will make you my last offer, twenty *quetzales* and fifty *centavos*. And that's only because business is slow today and you are very *simpático* and I like you."

The buyer hesitates. "Really, I swear by the Virgin Mary all I can pay you is twenty *quetzales*. But I am paying in gold. You know that is really worth at least twenty-one *quetzales*. You will get a premium."

"Ay, Señor, you are taking the *tortillas* out of the mouths of my children. You really have a hard heart. But what can a poor soul do?"

She makes a package, using an old newspaper and tucking the ends in cleverly.

Antonio speaks up for the first time.

"My husband," María hastily puts in.

"Ah, yes," says the buyer. "You have a fine little wife. She is a good business lady."

"Señor, you speak the truth. We are honorable people, too. But I must make a special appeal to you to add a few pieces of silver—at least enough for a little *tragito*, a swallow to moisten the throat, and to buy a few *dulces* for the children."

"By paying gold, I have already overpaid you," replies the buyer sternly. "I have made the bargain. The transaction is completed." He slaps down the two gold pieces.

Antonio looks at them sadly. "You know very well we can't spend gold."

"What do you mean?"

"Gold is to be buried."

Each Maya, it seems, has his own little hidden gold mine.

With the demand for Mayan fabrics in the cities and from tourists, the market has grown, and today, many towns now have small mills with half a dozen to ten looms. They are of the same primitive sort that Antonio uses, but hired hands do the weaving. They must work much harder than he does, and enjoy fewer breaks for a smoke.

Cotton-weaving has disappeared in many places. In ancient times, the people wore cotton from the silk-cotton tree. Later, regular cotton came in. The work has always been very beautiful; the rainbow colors are a delight. But after the First World War, the Germans found that by duplicating the colors and imitating even the defects of hand-weaving in machine-made products, they could make a profit by competing with the local craftsmen. So today, a good part of the cloth is no longer made in the home.

Still, since styles in dress differ from village to village, there remains much demand for the homemade product. Indeed, most Guatemalans can tell from the garments and the hat of a traveller what village he comes from, what his status is, and what he does for a living.

Local artisans turn out intricately designed tapestries, cross-stitching, tufting crepe, and netting.

But tourists, ruled by their own tastes, are, usually, unappreciative of native artistry. They are thinking of how a certain tapestry will look as a rug in their own homes. Thus, the tawdry goods go to market, and the best are kept for use at home. Tourists have unknowingly diminished both the quality and the beauty of Guatemalan art. The designs that repeat the ancient motifs relating the legends of the birds and the animals, the priests and the warriors of the past are dear to the Guatemalan heart, but beyond the experience of the average tourist.

The *huipil,* or blouse, of the women also varies from place to place. Usually it is made of a single piece, with a slit for the head to pass through, and caught together under the arms by thread or a brooch. But in Aguascalientes, it is made of two pieces sewn on both sides. The more sophisticated blouses of Cobán are made from three pieces. The length of the *huipil* also varies. In Palín, the blouses do not quite reach the skirt so a strip of skin is revealed; often a net is used which gives a peek-a-boo effect over the skin beneath. In highland areas, the *huipil* is quite long; in some places, it is tucked under the skirt, and in others, left to hang free. In the mountain villages, as in many places on the coast, it hangs well below the knees

Woman with rolled "halo"

like a smock. In colder places, such as Jilotepec and Chinaca, several *huipiles* are worn for warmth. Nearly everywhere, they are heavily embroidered.

The woman's cape is usually of a rectangular, brightly colored fabric, although sometimes, it is of a solid yellow, brown, blue, or red cloth. It can be folded over the head, neck, and shoulders for protection against the sun, or coiled into a ropelike circle to cushion jars of water and other heavy objects carried on the head. In Santiago Atitlán, the head is encircled by a narrow band, or rolled cloth, almost like a halo. The women of Senahú use a false queue or plait of orange wool.

Girl with silver filigree necklace, Alta Verapaz

Man from Sololá with typical skirt

Various towns are famous for their special wares, such as Sacatapequez for its *huipiles* and San Raimundo for fringed head coverings. (Brides and virgins wear special head coverings.)

The chief article of jewelry is the necklace, which also indicates the wearer's village and status. It can be silver filigree from Alta Verapaz; jade; coral; seed, glass, and metal beads; silver coins of many ages and of many countries; or animal teeth. Even the men wear jaguar or crocodile teeth as symbols of their own personal prowess, and as talismans against disease.

Often the men's trousers are very baggy, almost like bloomers, and in Sololá, might actually be a short skirt. The customary sash is nearly always red, but it may occasionally be magenta or striped. The men of Aguascalientes wear short blue jackets. The jackets of the Chile Verdeans are gaudily embroidered, and sometimes are decorated with sequins. In San Marcos and San Pedro, shirts, often partly silk, are mostly a gay orange or yellow.

In Chile Verde, the men wear outfits almost like priests' robes with foot-long bright fringes at the very bottom. Over these are worn sleeveless woollen capes that reach below the knees. A turbanlike headdress flows halfway down the back. Some Chile-Verdean men wear very grotesque white-and-red striped pantaloons that flare at the ankles. In Aguacatán, an embroidered long-tailed coat with many ornamental buttons is popular. The San Pedro Sacatapequez jacket is always bright red. In many places, the men wear a large sunburst over the chest or stomach to indicate at least former noble status.

Embroidery is generally done by the men and not by the women. Everywhere, men carry knitting bags. During free moments, they make *henequén* bags and nets.

For fiesta wear, or Sunday-best, the San Cristóbal women attach to the necklines of their dresses bertha collars embroidered with flamboyant flowers. In Cobán, a bertha of lace is preferred. The fiesta *huipil* of Totonicapán is dark blue with tufts of loosely twisted silk. It is sewn with different-colored silk threads, and sometimes is trimmed with *randa*, strips of colored lace. Their widths vary according to the worth in worldly goods of the wearer.

Dyeing is an important industry everywhere, whether done in the home or commercially. Formerly, only vegetable dyes were used, but artificial and mineral dyes are imported now. Various techniques are used to set the colors of vegetable dyes; in Momostenango, the dyed cloth is soaked in the adjacent hot-sulphur springs. At the shore, men wade out to sea and stain threads or fabrics a royal purple on the spot with mollusks scraped off the stones.

There is the usual division of work. Women also weave but on a simpler loom hung from a rafter or a pole and held taut with a belt, the spindle dancing madly meanwhile in a bowl. With just a couple of smooth sticks and a pile of yarn, they can turn out amazingly intricate designs. Their finger-weaving imitates embroidery. Designs are usually personal ones such as symbols of the weaver's family, her tribe, or her caste. The designs are, to a certain extent, conventional. Many of them were established perhaps generations before, and include many old motifs: the sun, the moon, the stars, lightning, corn, agave, chili, and flowers; deer, rabbits, jaguars, crocodiles, owls, *quetzales*, parrots, macaws, turkeys, and the plumed serpent. Two-faced eagles and double-headed doves are used to represent a two-faced god. Other deities are depicted, too. Human figures appear often; the figures of warriors or priests, often with elaborate feather headdresses or robes, abound in the complicated designs.

4 *Bananas and Boats*

Quiriguá is not as striking as most Mayan ruins. It is a place of carved *stelae,* or stone columns, on which have been inscribed in fine patterns and heavy hieroglyphics, the ancient legends of the Maya and his fellow creatures. But most of the columns have been tossed down and lie in the tropic rot.

Yet, here are a few ancient chapels and some of the finest art work the Mayas ever did of plumed serpents, jaguars, a huge stone tortoise, and many unidentifiable animals or curious fanciful combinations of men and animals. The friezes of human figures, of leaves, and of flowers are exquisite. The outlines, rounded and flowing, are more graceful, and the carving deeper than at Copán or Tikal. The faces are individualized portraits, strong, serene, and beautiful.

Quiriguá belongs to an early Mayan period. The region was probably settled and developed by Mayas who came down the Motagua River from Yucatán.

It lies in a seventy-five-acre reservation set up and maintained by the United Fruit Company, which at least cuts down some of the tropical growth. It is reached by a small gasolineengined car over narrow-gauge banana tracks. For this is the "capital" of the entire banana world of Central America and the Caribbean. The company which ships out bananas to the whole world is known as *La Frutera*, and the United-Fruit center here is called Bananera. There are, however, banana camps and towns all along the lower stretches of the railroad from Zacapa to Puerto Barrios. Many other peoples have been brought in by the company; Jamaican Negroes, Chinese, *mestizos* (persons of mixed blood). Bananera has become a melting pot of many races.

Bananera does not seem to belong to Guatemala at all. It is more like a tiny benevolent kingdom set in the jungle in the midst of farflung banana fields. Its houses and buildings have little in common with the others in the land. An ugly yellow, they have tin roofs, almost deadly in this land of relentless sun. Even those lived in by the better-paid foreign employees are without charm. The outsiders, who live in a large compound enclosed by barbed wire, have the same kind of yellow houses, but they are larger and have screened-in verandas.

It is the Mayan banana-pickers that we wish to visit. Not all the Mayas who raise bananas live at Bananera. Some either rent or have their own small plantations far away, or work for large Guatemala-owned plantations.

The Mayas and some other workers, live well down the main railroad tracks in their own settlement. Most of their yellow houses are built on stilts for coolness and protection from insects, animals, and floods. They are encouraged to use mosquito netting, too, for this is a deadly malaria country, and none of their homes is screened.

The big two-hundred-bed hospital has carried on much research in both the prevention and the cure of tropical diseases. Hookworm, which used to be widespread, has been largely eliminated. Some of the diseases are unknown in more northern climes.

In this land, there are many plant diseases also, and some attack the banana. Intensive studies have been made of such

Plantains for sale

diseases. The worst, for which no certain prevention or cure has ever been found, is a root blight. When it hits, fields have to be abandoned for long periods, and then entirely new, healthy plantings have to be made. (Much of the United Fruit Company's land is converted to the growing of cacao or cattle-raising.) Much research has been done toward the improvement of agricultural methods, fertilizers, pruning, and general care.

The banana is the largest of all herbs. It does not bear seeds, but is propagated from root cuttings or from corms. Within the triangular corm, which is like a callous, the entire tree develops in miniature: roots, stalk, leaves, or fronds, and tiny fingers that will become bananas. As the corm separates from the mother plant, the future tree develops inside it; leaf after leaf unfolds until they droop down as in the grown tree. The purple flowers are large and heavy. The banana fingers are pointed upward in little whorls, but once mature, they hang down; their leaf-green turns to yellow and then black when finally ripe. The banana eaten from the tree, like most fruits, is far more delicious than those picked green and allowed to ripen separately or in bunches.

There are many kinds of bananas, ranging from the tasty tiny ones, three inches long, which are sold in local markets, to the huge plantains, good only for cooking. Often red before ripening, some plantains are more than a foot long and as plump as baseball bats. Only a few varieties of bananas are marketed in the United States.

Once the tree has given its yield, it must be cut down to make way for one of its selected shoots or a new planting. There are about five hundred trees to an acre, although the soil and weather conditions may reduce, or increase, their average. The growing tree requires constant care. It must be kept free of undergrowth, which saps the soil and is a fire hazard. It must be pruned and inspected meticulously. The elements—floods, storms, and hurricanes—can bring with them vast damage; a hurricane can flatten a whole farm. The difficulties are legion.

Most of the fruit ripens at nearly the same time, which

demands quick action and many hands. The fruit must be cut when it has reached maximum size but while it is still green. The average bunch of bananas has about 175 bananas. These bunches, which can weigh as much as seventy pounds, must be handled carefully so as not to injure the fruit. One man climbs the tree and cuts the bunch down; another catches the stem; a third places it on the cart; a fourth drives a load off to the narrow-gauge railroad. Still other men load the fruit carefully onto heaps of greyish half-dried banana leaves which cushion the fruit during its trip to Puerto Barrios, the banana port on the Atlantic side. Once there, it is loaded on the company ships with great care. To reduce handling and possible injury, much of the loading is now done by power lifts. The bananas must be delivered unharmed to corner groceries in the United States just as they are beginning to yellow. Such is the life history of the prized Gros Michel, the variety to which North American buyers are accustomed.

In Guatemala, much of the labor, especially the seasonal kind, is paid on a piecework basis. Occasional cutting is done all year round, but its peak lasts three months. A worker, it is claimed, can earn four or five dollars a day during this season. Actually, few make more than $1.25 a day, and most of them, less. The remainder of the work period is for only three or four days a week so that the average weekly wage remains low. The workers who are not all-year-round men are unemployed much of the year and, as a result, suffer much deprivation. With no other industries nearby, they live off credit against the next season's work granted them by the company stores.

The life here is fairly good for many, but as an organized commercial operation it has little of the color of the coffee country. Here the Mayas abandon their colorful dress; they are just workers in blue jeans, and their women wear shapeless store-bought calicoes.

But they sing at their work, and they string hammocks around the raised houses and strum their guitars. Even so, the old-time culture is dwindling away. The old music, legends,

These boys are plantation workers

Coast jungle, Quintana Roo

and religion are almost forgotten. Their roots have been cut, and they have taken on many of the characteristics of factory-workers everywhere. What they have lost in the transition cannot be replaced.

The Mayas of the banana lands, and their fellow workers, send on their way abroad from four to seven million stems of bananas every year, an effort from which the Government collects around $100,000 a year in export taxes.

On the northern shore of Belice, a Maya is squatting under a tree of breadfruit, a large melonlike green fruit that has an insipid taste but is widely eaten. He is making a fish trap out of bamboo and hardwood. It is a simple affair: A large opening gradually narrows to an inner outlet by means of sticks whittled to points at that end so that the fish cannot easily retrace its path. He binds the slatted bamboo together cleverly with tough lianas.

To catch a shark, a Maya will use a long rope on the end
of which is tied a short hardwood stick that has been sharpened
at both ends. He buries the stick in a piece of fresh meat. A
swimmer carries this out beyond the surf, and when the shark
swallows the meat, the sharpened ends of the stick dig into
the sides of its mouth. The shark is in such agony that it can
no longer struggle. It is easily pulled in and then killed with a
club or knife.

The kill yields food—for the flesh of the shark is eaten—and
valuable by-products. The innards are believed to have magical
curative qualities. The skin is made into gloves, shoes, and
other such necessities. The teeth are cherished for amulets
and necklaces; they are used also for the pointed ends of darts
and hunting spears. Many fish are caught by spearing, a method
used in both fresh and coastal waters.

The Mayan boatmen on the inland rivers generally use
dugouts, some of which are quite large. On the coast, the
Mayas have learned to make boats with board planking, which
they bend by means of heat and other processes, peg together,
and caulk. Much drumming, chants and soothsayers' prayers
accompany the selection of the proper tree and the business
of cutting it down, dressing it, burning out the insides, and
smoothing it down with machete and sand. Sometimes, for
additional assurance, the finished boat is even blessed by the
priest.

> "Sail safe and sure, my fine boat,
> Take me through the rapids,
> Keep clear of the rocks,
> Ride high, ride sure, ride proud,
> My good boat. Take me swift
> To my sweetheart. Take me swift to my home.
> Carry me home to my children."

So sings the boatman. Usually, a dugout is manned by two
boatmen—one at the bow and one at the prow. Standing up,

each wields a long, sweeplike oar, thus making fairly good time even against the current.

The boatmen in their cotton shirts, short trousers, and bright sashes are important people on the rivers. They carry passengers and freight.

Among the important loads they carry is brown sugar, used by nearly everybody. All along the rivers, such as the Usumacinta, Hondo, and Copán, there are small *trapiches*, or presses, for extracting the juice from sugar cane. These are usually hand affairs of homemade wooden rollers with iron cranks. The canes are fed in between the rollers. The juice that runs off through a trough to a wooden tank is boiled down, usually in large terra-cotta receptacles, poured out when the proper concentration has been reached and the crushed cane stalks fed to cattle or pigs. Later, the brown sugar that has been thus obtained is broken up into hard chunks, which are tied

Boatmen

up in burlap, or banana leaves, for transport to various river settlements and towns. Sometimes the loads of *panocha* are so big that their weight sinks the dugouts almost to the gunwales.

The boatmen carry many other products, among them exotic fruits such as papayas, mangoes, avocados, breadfruit, pineapples, and chirimoyas. The chirimoya is a large fruit with a green skin embossed with scalelike markings; its sweet-tasting flesh, almost white and scattered throughout with small black seeds, has a granulated texture, almost as if sprinkled with sand. The taste is difficult to describe; it has been likened to a vanilla ice cream mixed with coarse granulated sugar.

The boats also carry bags of rice, a staple product everywhere; dried corn, either on the cobs or shelled; salt, in great demand; and scores of other commodities such as onions, chilies, tobacco, coffee, textiles, sombreros, machetes, knives, candles, paraffin, beeswax, pottery, and grinding stones. Perhaps the greatest human comfort they bring is the messages from friends and relatives up and down the river and in the villages. And, like local newspapers, they keep the isolated peoples along the stream informed on what is going on in the world. The Mayan boatmen are important indeed.

5 Men of God and the Healers

Father Benjamín Morazán, who bears the name of a much beloved former president of Guatemala, stands in his black robe at the top of the steps in front of his little church in Chahul, Quiché province. His broad, friendly smile has a touch of solemnity, for it is the day of the blessing of the animals. The little plaza is jammed with people who have brought their animals scores of miles.

All the previous day, the people have been busy decorating their animals. The animals are painted in such bright colors and combinations of colors as white, red, yellow, blue, and green. Bold patterns of stripes, circles, and zigzags are not uncommon. One thin horse has a white bull's-eye painted on one side; golden rays radiate from it along the moving horse's flank and neck and toward its legs and head. There is a mule that is striped like a zebra. On a few creatures, the colors have begun to run.

The animals' ears, necks, and legs are hung with cockades, ribbons, rosettes, and little bells that tinkle when they stamp their feet. The chickens cluck nervously; the cows moo forlornly; the dogs bark and snarl; the pigs grunt; and the sheep bleat.

As the owners carry, lead, or pull their animals forward, Father Benjamín murmurs his blessing and scatters a few drops of holy water on each. Now and then, he makes a joke or inquires about family or crops. As the heat mounts, his comments grow less frequent and he occasionally sighs wearily.

"Be careful, Padre," says one peasant, bringing up a mule, "Don Pancho here bites."

But the mule does not bite this time. He, too, is hot and weary, and wears what might be mistaken for a holy expression.

A cat, in the arms of a pretty girl, proves difficult. The animal does not like even holy water. "Thank you, Father. Niñita is usually so good." The girl drops a coin in the metal container rattled by a neophyte in a white lace surplice that by this time, has begun to rumple.

A favorite tale is that of the *gringo* (American) coffee buyer who was passing through the town the day before the blessing. He had been drinking in the local tavern when a dog painted green with pink polka dots ran in under the swinging door. He gulped, hastily called for another drink, and wiped his forehead nervously. Just as he was finishing it, a purple dog with yellow stripes and circles trotted into the bar. It is said that the *gringo* crossed himself and collapsed. He had to be carried up to bed. A doctor was called to his bedside. "I don't need a doctor," the *gringo* whispered, "I need a priest."

The tale relates that, from that day on, the *gringo* never again touched strong drink.

"Thank God," he is reported to have said afterward, "I didn't see a pink elephant. But what is worse, those dogs were real dogs. It was just that their colors were so strange. I'd had only one drink. Do you think. . . ."

The day of the blessing of the animals is very dear to Guatemalans. They have just as much fun then as North Americans do when coloring Easter eggs or turning themselves into witches and ghosts on Halloween. If a Maya saw a Halloween

Easter procession, Antigua

ghost while visiting the United States, perhaps he, too, would faint.

Father Benjamín has many other duties besides blessing the animals. He must be up before daybreak to celebrate Holy Mass every day in the week.

He must hear confessions, visit his parishioners, seek out and minister to the sick. His services are called for at all births, baptisms, christenings, weddings, and funerals. His duties are especially heavy during Lent and Easter and at Christmas.

Father Benjamín's attendance is required, too, at each of the many festivals that celebrate the birthdays of the various special saints; with the church elders, he heads the procession. These fiestas are great, prolonged celebrations. The statue of the saint being honored is taken out of the church and paraded through the village. The streets resound with the rhythms of drums, *marimbas,* or flutes made from either human, or animal, bones. Clowns whip through the crowds of praying, hymn-singing, or dancing participants. There are even speech-making politicians moving through the procession.

Sometimes the procession goes on to nearby villages. In years past—all that is ended now—pitched battles sometimes occurred when the peoples of other villages brought out their own saints. After a great clamor disputing the superiority of the rival saints, the competition would often degenerate into outright name-calling. A blow would be struck, and suddenly, everybody would be fighting. Since they all carried machetes, some of the combatants would be badly wounded, at times fatally. The women usually fled, although on occasions they, too, joined in the dreadful melees. Usually, the authorities were helpless, and only priests like Father Benjamín could stop the rioting.

Father Benjamín also has to travel widely. At least once a year, but usually more often, he must visit settlements where there is no priest. This requires long trips on horseback to small places in the mountains deep in steep *barrancas,* or hollows, along the rivers. There he holds services and will baptize and marry, sometimes en masse. Dead souls must be rescued from purgatory; the sick and infirm, blessed and comforted. Meanwhile, he endures many hardships, eats food he does not like and gets indigestion, sleeps in bad quarters, sometimes without a bed although usually there is a clean mat or a new hammock for him.

Father Benjamín is quite a scholar: He knows Greek and Latin and has read all the great religious works and the classics. He can hold his own in any urban intellectual gathering, but except for a rare visit to Guatemala City, seldom has the opportunity.

At home, he lives in a small, three-room adobe house. It is nicely furnished; he even has a fine radio set. His manservant is a Maya who moves stiffly in ready-made clothes and scuffed tan shoes.

Over the wine and biscuits he serves to visitors on a silver tray, he explained his way of life. "Yes, I live considerably better than the townspeople. But I share their lot on my trips or whenever it is necessary. It is not that I desire to be above them or free from their troubles. But unless I have the proper rest and peace of mind, a place for quiet meditation free from petty irritations, I cannot serve them as well. And also I must live in a way that gives them an example of how to be more civilized—the sort of life they could live if they desired it."

The door to his bedroom was ajar. "Ah, yes," he said, "you are looking at the lace pillows piled high on my bed and the lace canopy. It is not something I like, but those things were made by the women of my congregation with patient loving fingers. They would be dreadfully hurt if I refused their gifts or got rid of them. How could I ever do that?

"In return, I do many things for their families, tell them how to keep their houses clean, how best to feed their children, how to improve their crops. I'm trying to persuade them to grow other crops besides corn. Anything will grow in this country, and they cannot grow enough corn per acre to provide them with the diet they should have. Until they grow other things, they will always be undernourished; they will always have strange diseases.

"Ah, my friend, I have studied and pondered such matters. To me, the people sometimes listen, as they rarely do to outsiders or government officials. They are a people who love their traditions and old ways. It is not easy to change them. These days, too, you have all these outside agitators who try to stir them up and sometimes do. No, their lot is not always a happy one. But perhaps it is happier than that of many men who are better off. Those who seek to help them are not always wise and often more enamored of their own mouth-noises and ideas than those to whom they direct their thoughtless words.

"No, sadly enough, not all priests are good men. How could that be? We, too, are human, though all of us, I am sure, try to live on a superior plane. But of these matters, Señor, I must not speak. All of us have our pride, as every man should have."

In the market, an herb woman spreads out her wares on the mat. She sets out piles of leaves, little bundles of leaves still attached to their stems, roots, seeds, powers, and charms. There are on display the red fingerlike blossoms of the "Hand of God"—the foxglove—from which the heart stimulant, digitalis, is derived. The plant and the drug, its dried leaf, are so named from the finger-shaped corolla of the flower.

Many of the native herbs, bushes, and trees provide medicines. There are leaves good for brews that soothe the stomach, induce sound sleep, or allay nervousness. Some are used for poulticing wounds or ulcers. Nasturtium leaves are pasted onto temples to help banish headaches caused by *"el aire,"* as they say. Sweat-inducing drugs are used to treat many ailments, among them respiratory difficulties such as colds, pneumonia, tuberculosis, and asthma. Quinine has become a standard preventive and treatment of malaria all over the world. There are concoctions for the kidneys and the liver; for rheumatism and arthritis; for pleurisy and epilepsy. The remedies for skin ailments are numerous. Indeed, there are few of man's maladies which are not provided for here.

Some people have said the herb woman also has secret potent poisons that will cause paralysis, loss of memory, even madness or slow death. Others are said to produce euphoria and laughter. There are many magical philters, love potions among them. This black art has been described in folk lore from earliest colonial days. Among the charms are "deer eyes," large polished black seeds with brown sections that make them look exactly like large liquid black eyes. How many of these are actual scientific remedies and how many mere superstition?

Mother with sick child

Accompanied by the proper hocus-pocus, the administration of some herbs probably does little more than improve the spirits of the sick by giving them hope. Yet, raising the hopes of a patient often gives him the strength to fight a disease. More and more, modern physicians are taking into account the importance of psychology to medicine.

The healers—often called medicine men by foreigners—are the Mayan doctors. They lean heavily on such psychological treatment and on the faith of the patient, yet appreciate the importance of prolonged hot or cold applications, massage, and salves, lotions, and poultices.

Mayas and bath house (temascal)

The *curanderos* also make use of steam baths. Few houses are without steam bathhouses where very high temperatures are produced by heating stones red-hot and pouring cold water on them. These baths are often followed by cold-water dousings and massages.

The healers will often prescribe pounding the body, switching it with green branches and leaves, or applying heavy pressures on it, presumably to drive out the evil spirit. Yet, such methods promote circulation. They are well-versed in the use of counter-irritants, which pull the blood, fever, and pain to a new, less dangerous center. At one time, it was the common practice for American doctors to inject turpentine at the critical peak of pneumonia; it drew the blood and fever to a different part of the body.

The Mayan healers have a whole repertory of mysterious hocus-pocus. They strew the sickbed with magical leaves, sometimes in magical patterns. They burn coconut oil and incense, reciting meanwhile special magical chants. With prolonged invocations, they will order the devil out of the body.

Among the Mayas, almost all sickness is ascribed to the devil or to an evil spirit, often summoned by the machinations of an enemy. Before a person can get well, the evil spirit must be checkmated or banished.

The patient's affliction is sometimes attributed to an illness in his *nagual*, or fellow soul, which may be either intangible or some animal selected for his *nagual*. This belief is known as totemism, and its followers believe that they are always accompanied by these companion souls; that their fates cannot be separated and that an evil or sickness afflicting the *naguales* means similar trouble for the persons themselves.

Sometimes the healer makes an incision and pretends to suck some animal out of the body. They have been known to resort to such trickery as producing small toads from their mouths. Often the offending creature supposedly extracted is buried with great ceremony.

Many of the *Ladinos*, the people of mixed blood, swear by

Midwife and sometime healer near Chichicastenango

the *curanderos* for the healing of many types of disease, especially wounds, gangrene, tumors, abscesses, and swellings of all sorts.

There are a large group of practitioners whose activities are similar to and complement those of the Catholic priest and of the healers.

The *brujos*, or sorcerers, male or female, are sought out for charms to insure a happy outcome in any of life's ventures—a business enterprise, a safe journey, a love affair, the crops, a new home—as well as to keep animals well and safe, ward off dangers, and outwit enemies and thieves. The *brujo* can strengthen a machete or some other tool. Most *brujos* are good people who really try to promote the welfare of their clients. But stories are told of evil ones who will bring about the sickness or even the death of a hated person by sticking pins into an effigy or burning an object belonging to the offending person such as a piece of his fingernail or toenail, or a tuft of his hair.

The soothsayers, a most important group in the village, will

Soothsayer and magic fire

go so far as to prophesy the outcome of a journey or other enterprise. These people perform their divinations with the old Mayan sacred calendar, still well-known to many Mayas. The horoscopes are closely connected with the ancient pre-Spanish 206-day holy year-cycle, consisting of twenty thirteen-day weeks. (The Mayan solar year is made up of eighteen twenty-day months, plus a "dead period" of five days at the end which are considered unlucky.)

Much magical computation by the soothsayers is carried on in connection with this calendar cycle, usually with the help of kernels of corn or other seeds. The soothsayer takes a handful, and from it, counts out the days. But he often makes his own rules or follows secret formulae known only to him; he will, for example, skip certain days. The result is a good or evil augury.

Six days of the month are considered especially malevolent, and a Maya avoids starting any enterprise on one of these days. He is also apt to change his plans if the outcome is predicted as disastrous. The soothsayer will request details of an itinerary and travel times and then warn the traveller of what places and at what times he may expect trouble or difficulties. Means are devised to offset this, or a whole new schedule is devised.

Another widespread group of professional prayer-makers, do not prognosticate; their function is to compose special prayers for all contingencies. Some apparently use native drugs that throw them into states of ecstasy and promote dreams and visions. The prayer-makers chant their prayers over and over to the persons consulting them, and sometimes will provide prayers for the persons themselves to use. He does not indulge in much magic beyond strengthening the faith that prayer can destroy evil and accomplish good.

Everywhere, these *brujos*, soothsayers, and prayer-makers come into inevitable conflict with trained doctors and with priests. The priests try to break down the superstitions of the Mayan people and to substitute for them a faith in the Christian God and the effectiveness of confession and priestly advice. In some instances, the priest steals some of the thunder of the soothsayers, just as the Mayan soothsayers borrow some Biblical and churchly ritual. They will combine well-known holy chants and phrases with their own promises, warnings, and cures.

Other aspects of the white man's urban culture also tend to break down the Maya's faith in his ancient spiritual leaders and healers. State schools, modern machinery, and propaganda from official quarters all contribute. Mayas who are conscripted into the army or who go off for a season or longer to work on distant *haciendas,* or plantations, are exposed to other cultures and ways of life. They are apt to come back with new ideas and alienated in part from their communities and the age-old ways.

6 Where the Hearth Fires Burn

In the hot country, a Mayan house may be a simple palm-leaf lean-to or a snug, well-thatched dwelling. In the high cold country, it is more apt to be built of adobe or stone.

Where the climate is hot, the house need be merely a protection against wind and rain. A temporary structure, which may become permanent, is made by stringing a strong liana line between two big trees and leaning palm leaves against it. This breaks the wind and provides a dry spot when tropical storms lash out. A further step is taken when palm leaves are leaned against the open side. This makes a natural tent with openings at both ends, although sometimes one end is closed up.

Ordinarily the Maya does not like his house too closed-in, for in the intense heat, any breath of air brings relief. Many a house is made of only four stout uprights, with cross-rafters above to hold a steep, thick thatched roof which will permit the rapid run-off of rain water. The sides may be completely open.

People go about with little clothing. Up to eight or ten

children often play naked in the house or yard. Men wear only shorts and sandals. Often women wear only a thin skirt and perhaps a kerchief that falls triangularly over their breasts.

The most common house is a rectangular building with a thatched hip-roof and wattled mud-daubed sidings. Sometimes the walls are not daubed so that more air can circulate through the bamboo or thin branches used as uprights for the walls. These are close enough together to give privacy. One can see the cooking fire through them but not the dwellers, except when close by.

A permanent house is not built without considerable thought and preparation. The location must be carefully chosen for level ground. Spanish houses are built flush with the street or the property line with the rooms facing an inside or back court. The Mayan house always has a front yard, often fenced in. It is more important that the location be flood-free and shaded from the sun by large trees than that it have a view or other charms. More important, the spot chosen must not have a curse on it or be haunted. And perhaps someone has

Palm-thatched house in Yucatán

Palm-thatched house

Under the ramada in the hot country

died there who would not want a house built. It would bring bad luck. So a soothsayer is called in to make a divination. The man, his wife, and their children pray together to the old gods, in the church, and on the proposed building spot.

Before doing anything else, the owner makes the house cross—of Mayan, not Christian, origin. In rare instances, he uses the family cross handed down for generations. The house cross is erected even before the building is started. Offerings of food, pottery, hallowed boughs and flowers are placed at the foot of the cross. The house is built around the cross. The cross, soon blackened with the smoke of burning incense and candles, is related to ancestor worship.

After the house has been built, an altar is constructed for the cross, which is supposed to remain there as long as the building stands. When the parents are gone, the empty house sometimes is kept up by the children to provide the cross with a home. When the old house collapses, a special small thatched structure or tabernacle may be built for the cross. Even if the land is sold, the cross is not disturbed and the relatives of the deceased retain the right to visit and pray there. Altercations sometimes develop. Former owners may protest because the buyer plants his corn too close to the cross. The cross must always be "fed" flowers and copal incense, and candles must burn before it constantly. A neglected cross is apt to communicate its resentment to neighbors and friends. Ill-feeling may arise in the community.

The days for beginning the cross and the house are carefully chosen. They must be "good days." The house must also be completed on a "good day." These days are selected by divination.

Once the proper day is chosen, a dawn prayer is said and the builder and his sons, relatives, and friends go into the woods to look for a nice white pine. No other wood can be used. They take along offerings of resin, copal, and candles to put before the selected tree. After the appropriate ceremonies and prayers, the lower branches are lopped off and the brush

Coastal Mayas, Rio Salado

cut away from where it will be felled, usually on the downhill side. Before raising the machetes to cut it, the group will recite a special prayer:

"Make thy heart big, oh, tree, here in the forest where thou growest, that thou may watch over us and guard us in our house."

Then, when the candles, resin, and pine sticks have burned up, the work begins. Two pieces are cut from the top part. The east side, which looks toward the place from where "our father, the sun, comes," is used for the face of the cross. The upright and the arms are squared and then mortised with much care by machete and knife; they may be nailed together later. When finished, the cross is set against a tree and further prayers are said with candles and copal. It is carried home in a sack so no outsider can see it before it is put in place.

With more ceremony, fruits and other food are placed before it. The altar is built as soon as possible. Every day thereafter, candles must burn before it.

For building the house itself, all the necessary materials are gathered before the work is started: timbers, light poles, bamboo, lianas for tying thatch. For ties, the bark of the *luc* is especially strong. The thatch may be long grass or palm or banana leaves. The grass is tied in bundles less than a foot long, which are then wrapped into cylinders about a yard long. Some three dozen bundles are required for each yard of house area, so even a small house will hold as many as two to three thousand bundles.

Usually there is a house-raising bee, though workmen are sometimes hired. Neighbors and friends pitch in to help. Lunch is served, usually with an alcoholic beverage. Either the owner pays for this or everybody contributes. Music is provided, and fireworks and rockets are shot off.

A special fiesta with more music and fireworks is staged when the peak of the roof is put into place. A really big fiesta marks the final completion of the house. Goats or sheep, sometimes a cow, are barbecued. There is much drinking, music, and dancing. This is the real house-warming. The soothsayer is always present and receives much courteous attention. The chief ceremony on this occasion is the placing of the cross on the altar and "feeding it" with the customary candles, incense, and gifts.

The clay between the wattled sides is put in later, often mixed with lime to make it more durable. It may be whitewashed. But sometimes, for better ventilation, the spaces between the upright poles are not filled in.

Nearly all houses consist of one room, although on occasion a partition is put in. Usually, a separate structure is built for cooking, since Mayan houses have no chimneys for the smoke. Food is prepared mostly over charcoal rather than wood. The firebox may consist of only a few stones placed to provide a better draw, but often it is built up into elaborate stovelike size, with grills and openings below for fanning the charcoal. The fans are sometimes just parts of palm leaves wrapped tightly at one end to make a handle. But some are made with great care and artistry. Many may be dyed or painted with floral designs or figures.

Charcoal-making is an important industry. In the dry season, on coming into a valley at night, the traveller often sees scattered fires far up the mountain slopes. They mark the kilns of the charcoal burners. These are located where there is a good stand of oak or other hardwood. It takes much skill and vigilance to make good charcoal.

Fences for the new home may be merely piled-up brush, stones, adobe, or dirt. But corrals for animals are usually made with stout two- to five-inch poles, with large posts, about four feet high, set at regular intervals. Sheep and pig pens are often made with heavier timbers and sometimes boarded up. The posts are not set so deeply as they are often moved. The horses are tied under thatched roofs, and the hayracks are made with poles.

Many houses also have *temascals* (an Aztec word), or sweat baths. The *temascal* is usually dug into the side of a hill on the grounds. Its outside is of adobe or stone. It is a small structure about six feet square with its floor generally lower than ground level. Inside, at one end, there is a corner fireplace, and at the other, a bench where the bather sits or lies. Because of the smoke, he does not enter until the fire has burned down to coals. The door, sometimes just a mat, is closed tight. The bather washes with hot water, then lies down and sweats. Or, he throws water on the red-hot stones for steam and is soon sweating profusely. Afterward, an old woman attendant douses him with cold water and massages him vigorously or beats his body with green switches.

Many houses, especially in the higher areas, are made of

Carrying loads of charcoal on the trail

adobe with steep, thatched four-sided roofs rising to sharp peaks. Wide overhanging eaves help to prevent erosion of the adobe and provide a front *ramada,* a sort of porch, sustained by four upright posts. Sometimes this is paved with stone. Frequently, these adobe houses are whitewashed or calcimined various colors.

Furnishings are simple. Woven mats are used as floor coverings, hangings, and beds. The food is usually served on mats. The diners sit cross-legged. To spoon the food from the terracotta dishes, they use *tortillas* rolled into trowel shapes, or help themselves with their fingers. Most Mayan families do have at least one knife and fork and spoon. But these are for *Ladinos* or foreign travellers, who are served on a low packing case covered with a tablecloth. A Mayan woman has been known to spread her headcloth for that purpose.

Occasionally, one finds low cane-bottomed chairs, sturdily made, although wooden benches are more common. Many people sleep in hammocks rather than on mats. The walls are bare but for an occasional bright mat, woven hanging, calendar, or picture of a saint, Christ on the Cross, or the Virgin Mary. A wheel of woven palm leaves, or some other such object with magical or religious purpose, might be found hanging on the wall.

Many houses have a *tobanco,* a slatted cradle slung from the roof in which such possessions as corn, unused clothing, fruits, and so on, are stored. Although it is almost unbearable if there is a smoky fire below, this is on occasion used as a sleeping place for guests. The *tobanco* is fairly inaccessible to rats, but it is a delight for tarantulas and centipedes, which often rustle above one's head in the roof thatch and occasionally drop down.

In the towns, many Mayas have become accustomed to living in tiled adobe houses with wooden or tiled floors. These are always thoroughly scrubbed each morning with a hollow cone of *henequén* fibre containing a piece of soap. The wooden floors usually acquire a yellowish tinge from a cleansing substance used in the water.

The kitchens have tiled braziers, since charcoal is practically the only fuel.

Often such houses are built on an L-shaped half-patio with an eight- to ten-foot adobe wall, calcimined some pastel color, dividing it from the adjoining house, which is similarly built. All rooms have interconnecting doors, but there are rarely any windows. Light and ventilation are provided by the patio doors which usually open out on a raised open corridor that is covered by a tiled roof; the corridor is flanked by a brick balustrade, usually with open-work designs of circles, diamonds, or other patterns. The front room, the *sala*, may have one or more iron-barred windows which open on the street, and the rear room may also have a barred window, if the house has a back corral or orchard. This last room, beyond the kitchen, is usually used as a bathroom. It is seldom fitted with a tub, but nearly always contains a shower. The floor tiles slope to a drain.

All windows and doors have inside shutters, which are hinged and can be folded into built-in spaces in the thick walls. Iron slots are attached so that the windows may be stoutly barred.

Clothes are washed at outside concrete or stone tubs. Sometimes a cooking shed equipped with a stove stands nearby. Usually, a charcoal shed is adjacent to the kitchen.

Some such houses have no inside plumbing, so the women or servants, if any, must tote water on their heads in large *ollas*, or pots, or in five-gallon oil tins, from the town fountain. It is amazing to watch these girls and women walking down the street with their loads so well-balanced on their heads.

The town houses are usually furnished more conventionally with tables and chairs, as the Mayas here have adopted certain European ways of living. The *Ladinos* or whites in such houses usually also have desks and sometimes small bookcases and cabinets. Also, they are apt to hang more pictures on the walls, although few of them are in good taste, being usually calendars or magazine cutouts. The occasional framed picture

Carrying water

is usually a family portrait or a religious picture, although one finds here and there a conventional landscape or picture of a well-known building or foreign street in Rome, Paris, or perhaps Sevilla.

The palatial *hacienda,* or plantation, homes of the wealthy are rarely lived in by Mayas except as servants. The construction and layout are similar to that of poorer dwellings. But there is elaborate iron-grilling on the beautiful staircases and balconies. The tiling, too, is much more intricate, both on the floors and along the lower parts of the walls. These often bear

Girl with basket on her head

"My parrot!"

attractive floral designs. Ceilings are always high, usually with brass openings in the corners for better ventilation. Those in the *sala* and dining room are frequently embossed with thick white or pink stucco with designs of fruit, flowers, cornucopias, or cherubs.

The balustrades are usually lined with finely glazed flower pots containing geraniums, begonias, roses, and other house plants. (Even the poor Maya nearly always has many flowering plants and vines growing in his home, even if the receptacles are mere tin cans covered with crepe or colored paper.) In the fine homes, the patios are always lavish with flowers, vines, shrubs, and perhaps a few trees. A fountain sprays a steady play of water into a tiled pool.

The Mayas usually have a parrot, macaw, or other such bird as a pet. The rooms and the patios of the wealthier homes are filled with bird cages, often gilded and expensive. Numerous songbirds are always singing cheerfully.

Every home has an altar or perhaps a chapel for family prayer just as the humblest Maya installs his family pagan cross at the time he builds his new home. The chapels of the wealthy contain more elaborate baroque altars than those of many public churches. In times of family, or national, crises, priests are called in to perform special masses for the family, relatives, and close friends.

7 *Woman's World*

Princess María Xuchal de Adam is a tall Mayan girl descended from an early Mayan king. She is married to a wealthy American sugar planter in Alta Verapaz. Sometimes she accompanies him to Guatemala City.

Her husband is a wise man who insists she continue to wear her Mayan dress although when in Guatemala City, she also will wear shoes, sometimes sandals, and stockings. She does not like shoes for they cramp her feet. Her clothes are of the finest materials. Her white blouse is embroidered with birds and flowers. Sometimes she wears clothes in rainbow colors that imitate the plumage of the rare *quetzal* bird. Her long smock comes to her calves, and the lace petticoat underneath reaches to her ankles. The expensive diamonds and rubies she wears have been worked into Maya-style earrings, necklaces, and bracelets. She wears her hair in typical smooth tight Mayan style, so setting off her small ears and accentuating the classical quality of her seemingly chiseled face. She is indeed beautiful. She carries her body with the erect grace natural to all her people. And she is proud—she never puts on European dress even for formal affairs.

Women at the market

The *Ladinos* of the capital despise the Mayas and their culture. The feeling is mutual. But since Princess María is wealthy and her husband an influential foreigner, she is accepted and sought after by high society who even feel honored if she accepts their invitations.

At home in Alta Verapaz, the princess prefers to go barefoot, as nearly all Mayan women do. The cool, smooth clean tiles of her home are pleasant underfoot. Besides, shoes are symbols of male superiority; they are the rightful prerogative of the male.

She lives on a great plantation in a handsome mansion with the customary high ceilings and an unusually ample garden patio, where a cool fountain plays constantly. The walls of her home have several niches for the statues of saints. She has many servants at her beck and call, all of whom love her and are loyal to her.

Not all Mayan women are so fortunate. Mayan men consider themselves superior to womenfolk. The wife—even the mother— is expected to show deference and to never speak out of turn. Yet, most Mayan families are hardworking cooperatives. Long custom has assigned each partner special, or joint, duties that he scrupulously performs.

The soil is cultivated by the men and the boys, but in some places, the women assist in the planting, the weeding of the fields, and getting in the crops.

Women do the cooking over the charcoal fires and wash the terra-cotta dishes. They grind the corn on the three-legged *metates* of stone and make the tortillas, a long, backbreaking task.

The men weave the wool; the women weave the cotton goods. Commercial weaving is mostly done by the men. It takes about three days to weave a blanket, light or heavy, with all its multi-colored wool yarn and designs. The women and girls assist in that they card and spin the wool yarn. It is carded with a currycomb set with metal or hardwood teeth, and is usually spun on a distaff. The men bleach and dye the wool, usually dipping it tightly bound to obtain many colors in addition to the natural white.

The men also do most of the knitting and embroidering, and also weave the palm leaves for hats and raincoats, although the women will sometimes participate in this.

The women do most of the marketing, especially for the products which require bargaining such as pottery, carved gourds, and woven goods. Men often purchase the more staple items such as corn, quinine leaves, *panocha*, or grain, and fruits.

The man also carries the flowers to market, arranges them, and keeps them freshly sprinkled. Both partners sell them.

"How much are the carnations?" a young woman asks.

"Seventy-five *centavos*, Niña."

"They are very nice, but I am broke this morning. I will have to buy fruit."

"A rich lady like you. . . ." The speaker, a buxom Maya in a loose calico dress, makes a clucking sound.

"It's true. I'm quite poor today. My allowance is all used up."

"It is sad to be poor even for a day." She pushes the carnations into the girl's arms. "Here, I give them to you because you like flowers so well."

"No, no!" protests the girl. "All right, I'll pay you tomorrow or next day."

"They are a gift, Niña!"

In some places, the woman also takes care of all the family finances, although she will hand over money unquestioningly when her husband asks for it. Elsewhere, all money may be held by the man, and the woman does not even have inheritance rights.

The woman cares for the children. Then, when they are about five or so, the father starts training the boys in farm work, fishing, and hunting, and she teaches the girls household duties. But some work begins for the child almost as soon as he can toddle. From the very first, children are accustomed to help with all the chores of the household and made to feel important doing so. If a woman brings in a load of wood, the child brings

in a tiny bundle or maybe just a single stick. From the beginning, they are treated not so much as children but as an integral part of their small world where each member, young or old, performs his duties to the best of his abilities or strength.

Some parents—like parents everywhere—are ill-tempered. But in most of the closely knit Mayan families, good humor prevails and punishment is rare. The opinions of the children

Opposite page: On the way to market

Mountain Mayas

A family on the way to work

are listened to and are often accepted in the making of family decisions.

As soon as a woman is with child, she and her husband make the rounds of the prayer-makers, *brujos,* and soothsayers, seeking advice and aid. As soon as birth pains begin, a midwife is called in. She feels the woman's body and announces whether it will be a boy or a girl. Usually, she is right! She will also prepare special foods and brews, and recite incantations and special prayers.

At the time of birth, the husband prays to the house cross and then goes outside where he continues to pray alone. He will return only after the child has been born. Again he prays at the pagan altar; then before a Christian saint, whom he solemnly informs of the event. He asks for blessing and assistance.

A soothsayer is summoned immediately to forecast the child's future. Will it live? What will its life be like? If the child happens to be born on a "bad day," there is great sadness. The soothsayer prays earnestly for its survival, about which he is very pessimistic. A child born on the sixteenth of the month is not expected to live long. This is the most evil day of the month, and in English, its name means "enemy" or "half-witch." Such a child is doomed, although some soothsayers claim they can overcome the evil influences.

The birthday may be arbitrarily set back or ahead, the pretense made that it was a "good day," and prayers said each month that the day recurs. Some soothsayers will also designate the child's *nagual*, its alter-ego and lifelong companion spirit and guardian. He protects it by blessing a certain rare ear of corn.

In some places, the mother starts to work right after the birth, but she usually remains quiet, doing little or no work, for twenty days or a full month. She prays constantly even when in bed. It is said that the midwife's knowledge and ministrations (she massages and bears down on the mother's abdomen) right after birth help to preserve the Maya's figure better than those of *Ladino* or white women. Also, the mother is required to take steam baths twice a day. The steam baths are to insure the quick recovery of good circulation and color. She is required to eat highly spiced foods and much *chile*.

She returns to normal life on the twentieth day. On this day, the husband holds the baby during long hours of prayer, for this is also the child's name day.

The child is not weaned before eighteen months are over, often not for several years. But they get other foods almost immediately.

The mother carries the child with her everywhere in a shawl on her back. There it sleeps, kicks, sucks its thumb, and stares at the world with enormous black eyes. It is put down only

Coming home from market with child in shawl

Piggy-back Mayan style

when the mother is performing sedentary tasks. It is fed whenever it cries.

If a boy, he is soon given a small machete that has been ground down from an old one and, as soon as he can, helps to cut wood and clear the fields. The little girls assist with housework. Both sexes are taught how to use the tump line to carry burdens. Their work is closely supervised.

Good manners are emphasized. Children must always cheerfully wait on their parents when asked. They are taught the old myths and tales and religious beliefs and kneel in prayer alongside their parents. There is great parental affection and pride, but the parents rarely display it.

Girls marry between the ages of thirteen and sixteen; the boys, a few years later. When a boy and girl become interested in each other, they show it in various conventional ways such as throwing twigs at each other, sharing fruit, and so on. In some villages, the boy breaks her water jar with a stick, thus dousing her. Her friends will rush in angrily to protect her and drive him away with stones.

Actual negotiations for marriage are carried on by the boy's father. After talking it over, they pray together at length. Early in the morning of one of the *oras*, or "best of days" such as the third, eighth, thirteenth, eighteenth and twentieth days of the month, the father rises very early to call on the girl's father. After much talk, mostly set and polite phrases having nothing to do with the proposed marriage, he takes off his hat and lays ten *pesos* (about ten cents) on it. The girl's father is obliged to pick up the hat and the money if he favors the match.

If he keeps the money, he names another *ora* for further negotiations. Meanwhile, he talks it over with his daughter. If she consents, the bartering begins. The price to be paid by the boy's family is usually between five to ten *quetzales*, each equal to the dollar and a large sum indeed for many peasants.

Once the negotiations have been amicably finished, the boy's father prepares for a great feast to which the girl's parents come. If he can afford to do so, the boy's father also builds a new house near his own place for the couple.

Promised mountain bride

Ladino *wedding*

The day after the big feast, the boy goes to the father-in-law's house to work for a week or longer. If his services are satisfactory, he takes the girl to his parent's home for a similar trial period. If her work is accepted, and she gets along well with her mother-in-law, the marriage is considered consummated. But if she is unable to bear any children, she can still be returned to her parents, who must then give back the bride money, and the marriage is formally annulled.

Before and after the marriage, the boy and the girl pray together periodically and confess their sins to each other.

A girl is trained by the mother

Among some Mayas, if the girl confesses to prior misdeeds, the boy may send her back to her parents. In most cases, conduct before marriage is not considered important; only that after marriage matters. If the couple have then been true to each other, if they honestly confess to each other and pray together constantly, they and their future children will be healthy and prosper. If not, it is believed that their children are doomed to death or terrible suffering. Most marriages are for life; divorce is very rare.

8 Fiestas

People are streaming into the churchyard for the big fiesta in Totonicapán, the mountain town which makes such fine embroidered blouses and shirts of silk. It is in the highlands and really cold country. Although the days are warm, the nights sometimes drop down to freezing temperatures, and there is no heat in any of the houses. "Icy but healthy," is the saying.

But no matter how cold, every evening the townspeople walk around the town's ornate iron-grilled kiosk. Music plays for the promenade. The girls walk in a clockwise direction, and the boys, the other way around, in the "flirtation walk."

It is a place of arcades and pink and blue and yellow walls.

Some of the people are Aztecs, whose forebears were settled here by the conquistador, Don Pedro de Alvarado, in the 16th century. That is why the town has an Aztec name. Totonicapán means "on the hot river," for there are famous hot springs nearby. They are often visited by people seeking health cures.

Even in Quiché days, the place was an important center. Here, twenty-five of the noblest families of the realm had their main residences. It was renowned in those days for its wood-

Big market day

workers, jewelers, potters, painters, and weavers. These arts still flourish in Totonicapán.

On this fiesta day in April, the big market has spilled over into the streets and plaza. Vendors are selling special candies, fruits, and drinks. Charcoal braziers glow red, and fill the air with the crisp spices of cooking food. Stands of multi-colored candles rise in tiers like pipe organs. Everybody must place a lit candle in the church.

On ordinary days, the workshops are open and busy. About half the shops, and homes, have a loom or two, and the shuttles fly across the big clumsy frames worked by foot-treadles as agile skilled fingers make intricate, balanced designs.

In open patios, whole families sit on the ground or the paving stones, modelling soft clay and shaping it into pots, bowls, and vases. One family specializes in tiny replicas of kitchen and tableware that are sold as toys for children. Rows of jars stand in the bright sun to dry before being put in the oven for glazing.

Elsewhere, tinsmiths are making receptacles, soldering pipes for drains, small cashboxes, or cylindrical tubes for documents. The carpenters in their shops, redolent with the pungent aroma of pine and of cedar, are busy making furniture, chests, and coffins out of these and other woods such as ebony, mahogany, and cypress. A little coffin, a child's, is being painted light blue with winged cherubs.

Other shops are turning out leather belts, bags, purses, and ornate saddles. The tanning of leather is an important local trade. A tanner can always be recognized by the permanent mahogany-brown skin of his hands.

Nobody is more respected than the mask-maker. He fashions

Family near Sololá

Family in the hot country

On ancient temple stairs in the morning mist

kindly and gruesome, comic and tragic masks of papier-mâché, wood, or leather to rent or to sell.

A local costumer sews dresses, costumes, and red skirts with sequins, glass beads, little mirrors, and shells for dances.

More and more people in bright clothes climb up and down the tilted cobblestone streets. They brighten the dark green foliage of the trails down the mountainsides. Most are in dance costumes, although they have not yet put on their masks. But there are also old folk (but not too old to dance), children, and sightseers from neighboring villages. With little white puffs of smoke, rockets burst noisily in the clear sky. A steady rapid *tom-tom* sounds from the church bell; it is being struck with iron bars.

Today is the Dance of the Little Bulls, or the Black Dance, as many Mayas call it. This dance, as are other "big" dances,

Flute player

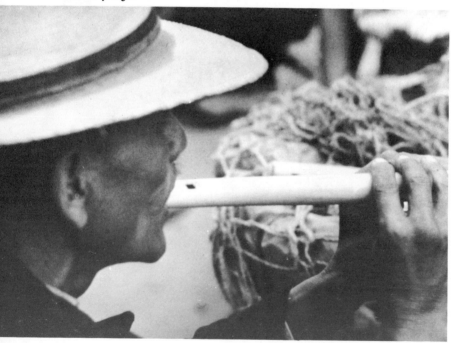

The drummers

is "owned" by a "master" who rents out the costumes and masks for it and also teaches the dance routines, which are rehearsed an entire year ahead of time on every *ora,* or good day. This is a family business, passed on from generation to generation. The master directs a sort of brotherhood, the members of which pay him a small fee. Membership is for life. The cost of renting the masks and costumes and of his services as director of the dances during the fiesta, which may last for days, is often more than $150, so smaller villages cannot observe a big fiesta perhaps for years. They have to celebrate it in simpler ways.

The people are impatient to begin. Still others will drift in as the fiesta goes on. The musicians start playing. There is no official *marimba* today, although a few are playing here and there to earn a few *centavos.* But there are many other instruments for the dance. The *xul* is a vertical flute that gives forth thin, piping notes. The *tzijolaj* is a small wind instrument. There are two kinds of drums, the *tun,* or *teponaxtl,* as it is called in Aztec, is made of the trunk of a hollowed tree; it has wooden languets which, when struck, give out a *boom* that can be heard for many miles. Symbolic figures and designs are carved on its highly polished exterior. There are also goatskin drums, more like the drums North Americans know. The *chirimía* is a clarinetlike instrument, and the *tot,* an incrusted shell-horn. The *chinchines* are the "jingles in gourds," that is, gourd rattles. (The music for this fiesta was recorded some time ago by Jesús Castillo, the famous Guatemalan musician.)

The players strike up a lively allegro, and the performance begins. The principal personages of the village—the officials, elders, prayermen, and soothsayers—greet and bring forward various actors. They are introduced and welcomed not only with great ceremony but with singing, too. The role of Torito, or "Little Bull," is played by a leading actor dressed up as a bull; the bull's mask and horns that he wears make him very convincing. He steps forward with the actor who is to represent the boss-man of the community, or *hacienda* owner, who is referred to in the play as "master."

The Toro's bullhide is made of mats on a curved frame. Two pieces of bright cloth are pinned to the back. His mask is made of real bull's hide, and a bull's tail is attached to his costume.

The troupe begins to dance. The two main protagonists go through their intricate steps and motions in the foreground. Behind them, the others form geometric patterns.

An allegro scherzo follows. The bull takes a back seat while the Mayordomo (or manager) and his Straw Boss perform the principal turns. They dance in lively fashion to the quick, spritely tunes of the gourd rattles.

The third act features the Dance of the Shepherds, which is a more sonorous one. The drums roll out their full steady beat, carrying the burden for the other instruments.

A famous Guatemalan artist, Carlos Mérida, has described how the flutes cut in: "The audience absorbed, and in ecstasy, feel in those flowing tones the blood of the race distilled into music."

The major theme, the lively Tune of the Torito, comes next. The master, playing the part of a toreador, goes through the graceful and agile movements of the bullfighter. Finally, Little Bull kills him. The music changes to a sad funeral march, mournful, full of pain. The instruments rumble and vibrate as the master is buried.

This is followed by the liveliest allegro of all. Spring returns. Life is renewed.

The dance lasts from four to five hours without a break. Nobody seems to weary.

All this follows ancient tradition, which has been described "as the tradition which sculptured Palenque and today embroiders with miraculous hands the marvelous shirts of Totonicapán."

Although the pastoral allegory is over, the music continues. The people go on dancing, breaking only to eat and drink, on into the twilight, on into the night as flickering *ocotes,* or pine torches, are lit. At dawn, the music still sounds, as if in answer to the early songs of the awakening birds.

There are many fiesta days. The New Year fiesta on March 14 celebrates the Day of the Bearers of the Year, when the ancient Mayan year begins. Another important event in the Mayan culture is the fiesta that marks the start of the 260-day religious year. The start of the Mayan solar year and of the sacred year coincides every thirteen years. This is a great event which calls for boundless celebration.

Religious procession

Ready for the blessing of fruits and flowers

Small children at a fiesta

It is a most solemn occasion that can be compared to the Christian Holy Week celebration on Palm Sunday. People bring flowers and fruits in new baskets to be specially blessed. Even in the markets, fruit and flowers are displayed on brand-new mats, which have been prayed over and sweetened by copal incense.

For the blessing of the fruit, a dozen or two slatted crates of perfect fruit are brought into a room hung with special flowers. A single candle burns on a table. At the proper moment, the fruit—bananas, pineapples, coconuts, mangoes, cacao, melons, chirimoyas, avocados—is removed gently from the crates. The fruit is carefully wiped and laid on new mats arranged in patterns. The marimbas play frenziedly. A censer with burning incense is swung. People are given *atole* in coconut shells, and afterwards fiery *agua* in little green glasses. (Glassmaking is another beautiful art practiced by the Mayas.)

There are many other important holidays. The Day of the Caves is a significant one, for caves are often sacred and fitted with altars and idols. Some are filled with offerings, or the ashes of offerings, that date back hundreds, perhaps thousands, of years. A special day admits the Christian village saint to the hierarchy of the old gods, an initiation that is repeated annually. On the Day of Rainmaking, special prayers and magical enterprises are supposed to make the god of rain generous.

A unique celebration is that of Sealing the Frost. It is observed in the hope of preventing damage to the new crops. The Frost is supposed to live in a crack in the face of a cliff. About the first of April, the people go with the prayer-makers to the edge of the cliff. There, by means of a rope, they let a prayer-maker down to the crack, which he seals up with mortar. Sometimes it seems as if it actually holds in the Frost. When the crops are attacked by frost, various explanations are given: The cliff had another undiscovered outlet, or the Frost was able to break out through the mortar.

The Day of the Village Boundaries calls for considerable ritual. But before the people can participate, the prayer-makers and the leading men of the village go to the head man and have him unlock the shrine in the town hall where the old village god is always kept hidden. They pray to the yard-high crude wooden figure. The throats of some turkeys or chickens are cut, small quantities put into two small gourds, and the rest burned with copal for a blood sacrifice. In the night, one gourd is taken to the top of the region's tallest hill, where it is placed on a rustic altar. Prayers are again said. If little green lizards come, drink the blood, and leave the bowl clean, all is well. The other gourd must be taken to a sacred cave and put beside a pool of water. If the water takes the gourd, cleans it, and returns it, it is a good omen. Otherwise, the prayers must continue, with even greater intensity.

After these ceremonies, the prayer-makers, followed by the whole village, proceed to all the high points around the town on which permanent boundary crosses are set. At each site, prayers are said for the village "and the whole world." Of course, the village is believed to be the center of the world and of true religion. Offerings are made to each of the crosses.

In addition to these traditional Mayan fiestas which go back to time immemorial, there are the newer Christian holidays: Lent and Easter; Christmas and the Day of the Kings when

Fiesta prayer-makers

gifts are exchanged; All Souls' Day, or the "Day of the Dead";
the Blessing of the Animals (taken over by the Church); and
birthdays, baptisms, confirmations, weddings. Wakes for the
dead are occasions for food, drink, music, and dancing. The
national Independence Day is always an important event. New
Year's Day of the European calendar is honored, too.

When holidays coincide—Easter with the Day of the Bearer
of the Year, for example—there is considerable confusion and
blending of events.

The dances of the Mayas—each with its own special music
heightening the excitement of the dance—are performed on
these days. They represent the creatures of the Mayan kingdom: the snake, the deer, the jaguar, the puma, the monkey, the
sloth. The Deer Dance, among the best dramas, portrays the
story of the hunter and the hunted. The dancers are costumed
in animal skins, realistic masks, and feathers. The music is
rather modernistic and very moving.

The snake dance, in which the rattles of rattlesnakes are
bound to the ankles, is executed with live snakes. They are
gathered under the guidance of a soothsayer. The venom is
drawn by teasing them with sticks and then their mouths are
sewed shut. They are brought into the plaza in jars and are
worn around the necks or other parts of the body by some of
the performers. This is a show-off dance, combining the talents
of half a dozen male performers wearing small black masks,
and a single woman in the usual Sunday-best *huipil* and skirt,
richly embroidered in silk. Her face is hidden by a red kerchief
held in place by a small grey felt hat. As each dancer jigs and
whirls, they take turns lashing at the others with a whip. One
dancer, with a long glowing feather headdress, carries an imita-
tion crocodile and snaps the jaws at the others. Sometimes the
dancers push the snakes into their shirt fronts and let them
writhe out the legs of their pants. There is much clowning.

At most of the festivals, there are always clowns who mimic
the serious dancers, try to trip them up, perform other foolish
stunts, and make ribald or witty remarks.

Impromptu clowning-dances take place frequently in the villages, apparently on no particular fixed date. One curious dance features two masked women in men's clothes and six men in women's clothes, their faces covered by kerchiefs.

All the Mayan villages perform a universal dance on their village saints' days which is, for them, a symbolic retelling of the Spanish Conquest.

Some participants are dressed as Spaniards with beards, armor, long lances. The turbaned Moors are always small men and a rather sad-looking lot. They enact a bellicose drama which took place far from Guatemala's shores years before the Spanish Conquest. The dancers and spectators really identify themselves with the Moors. Throughout the dance-drama, the Moors have the advantage. The Spaniards are repeatedly overborne, routed, reviled, and mistreated. But the lugubrious concession to historical reality is made at the end—usually with sad and forlorn music—when final victory for the Spaniards is granted.

This, and other important, dances are rehearsed in private on the *oras*, or good days, throughout the year. Besides the regular professional dance director, the Master, there are special brotherhoods of "Captains" who keep the costumes and masks; they volunteer their services for the entire year. On the day of the fiesta early in the morning, the Captains visit the homes of the dancers to see that the costumes fit and are worn properly. They are given bread, coffee, drinks and gifts.

Before the dance begins, the leading performers, and even the ordinary participants, pray and whip themselves before the family cross with leather thongs that have sharp splinters of glass imbedded in gobs of wax on the ends. A special attendant wipes off the blood. This is said to be a precaution against rain ruining the fiesta.

The first day of Lent is preceded by five continuous days of fiesta. The *toro* dance goes on all five days and then is repeated every Sunday during Lent. Lent is a period of many processions and much music. The marimbas play day and night. In one highland procession headed by the priest, his assistants, and neophytes, as many as forty saints are carried. But an old man in the rear carries a pagan idol in a blanket. Inside the church, there are special ceremonies amid flowers under a canopy.

In most fiestas, there is always a period when the people enter the church and dance before the altar and the saints. If it happens to rain, the people crowd in suffocatingly.

Holy Thursday is the day the people prepare to burn Judas on the next day, Good Friday. The people, wearing Judas masks, clown and play tricks all day. The children never cease beating their small drums, shaking gourd rattles, and twirling their *maltracas,* or Judas bone-breakers, as they run in and out of the church.

The *maltraca* is an instrument with taut wooden slats over a ratchet. As the ratchet turns, the slats slap down; the faster the toy is whirled, the louder its harsh smacking sounds. It is also used on the Day of the Dead.

Early in the morning of Holy Thursday, the constables round up young men to go out and bring in a tall pole on which to hang Judas. Others set to work preparing the effigies. That made by the sacristan and his assistants is usually the most elaborate. It is dressed in European clothes complete with a hat, a wooden mask, and tan shoes. Then it is stuffed with straw, candy, sugar cane, fruit, toys, and clothing. Strings of firecrackers are often attached, although this ruins the costume. At 3:00 P.M., the finished effigy is placed in a chair at the church door for the crowd to jeer at.

Other Judases are made by the *Cofradías,* the lay religious groups. This is done ceremoniously with crucifixes and candles around the walls. The women, in red headdresses, sit on the floor, and the men wear red kerchiefs, too, with the ends knotted behind their ears, and black capes. Copal is burned. The image is dressed in half a dozen shirts, trousers, and many colored sashes. Two hats, one inside the other, are set on his head. A big black cigar is stuck in his mouth.

The Judases are strung up by the necks at about ten o'clock

Judas aloft

the next morning. They dangle until mid-afternoon before the church, in the plaza, and elsewhere in town. As the firecrackers explode and the gifts start spilling out, the children rush in to grab them. A tremendous mix-up! To add to the hilarity, the burning Judas is lowered and raised. The really big scramble begins when the Judas, half torn apart, is finally lowered to the ground.

On Saturday of Glory, the fun-making reaches its peak. A

clown-dance is held. This usually gets entangled with the Dance of the Little Bulls. The music of both groups plays, neither band playing the same tune. The rockets explode on high. The church bells ring incessantly. The *maltracas* "break the bones" of Judas. People sing and shout and dance. It is a terrific uproar that must wake the dead. It is indeed a time of resurrection.

9 The Making of the Mayas

From whence came the Mayas? Scholars keep pushing their history further and further back into antiquity, as far back as five million years ago.

The *Popol Vuh*, the Book of the Quiché, which contains both legend and history, recounts three myths of creation. One takes the story back to the days when the land still lay beneath the sea. According to the *Popol Vuh*, Guatemala, as one of the earth's oldest land formations, finally emerged from the ocean as a block of granite. In time, it became populated with, among other creatures, dinosaurs and great mammals.

The *Popol Vuh* tells how before this geological change occurred, the god, Gucumatz, and the folk hero, Tepeu, lived on the endless black sea in a little circle of light:

"All was silence, everything motionless, not a sound, and the whole expanse of the sky was empty . . . Nothing could be heard, nothing moved, nor stirred, nor a whisper from the sky . . . There was only calm water, a still sea, alone and tranquil."

The two gods were adorned with brilliant feathers from the

Mountain scene

plumage of the *quetzal*. (It has since become the national emblem of modern Guatemala and a symbol of freedom for it dies in captivity.) They consulted with Huracán, whose name meant Hurricane, or "The Heart of Heaven." He was the one-legged god of thunder and lightning and storms. They chose him to push aside the sea.

"Do it," he was told. "Fill the emptiness. Let the waters retire and cease to occupy space. Let the earth rise up. Let there be light on earth."

Huracán cried, "Earth! Earth!" Instantly, it was formed.

"Creation was like a mist, like a cloud, like a storm of dust, when the mountains rose from the water. In an instant the mountains grew." The valleys and rivers were formed.

"There will be no glory or grandeur on earth till the human creature, mankind, is formed," said one god.

The next day Huracán created the guardians of the mountains—the deer, the birds, the lions, the tigers, the serpents, the snakes, the vipers—and the guardians of the *bejucos*, or vines.

"You, deer, sleep on the fertile shores of the rivers and in the ravines. There you will live among the thickets and the plants. There in the forest you will multiply. On four feet you shall walk and be supported."

They told the birds, the big ones and the little ones, where to live. "In the trees and vines you shall make your nests. There you will multiply. There you will flutter among the trees and vines."

But none of these creatures could be encouraged to speak. They screamed, cackled, and cawed without a sign of language. Each one cried in a different way. How could they speak the names of the gods who had created them?

"How will we be remembered on earth?" the gods asked.

"Let us make beings, who will be obedient and respectful," said one.

So they made man out of mud. Without strength, it could not move its head, its face went lopsided, it could not see, it could not walk. Moreover, it could not speak; it had no sense whatever. It was a crude job and the creature, too soft, soon fell apart and became watery. Clearly, such a creature could not multiply.

The gods held a big cabinet meeting. Present were Tepeu, Gucumatz, Huracán, and all the others. They summoned Twice the Mother; Twice the Father; the Lord of Emeralds, Sculptoring, and Carving; the Lord of Beautiful Dishes; the Lord of the Green Gourd; and the Lord of Resin.

The grandmother and grandfather gods made a divination with corn and *tzité* seeds from the century plant, the agave. They learned that they should create a new man out of wood. All agreed.

It was done. The new wooden men spoke and conversed. They had children. They multiplied. But they had no souls, no understanding. They could not remember their creator. They ran about aimlessly on all fours like cats.

"Well, it was just a try, an attempt to make man," the gods sighed.

At first, it had seemed a success. But without blood and substance, the yellow flesh of the cheeks, hands, and feet of the wooden men were dry and stiff. Although they filled the earth, what good were they without the power to express themselves? The gods decided to destroy them. They brought forth a great deluge.

Again, the gods tried to make man. They made the flesh of man out of the *tzité* or agave, and that of woman out of cattail plants from the marshes.

But these new beings could not talk with their creators, and after torturing them terribly, the gods destroyed them, also. First hot resin fell from the skies. Then one god put out their eyes. Another cut off their heads. A third devoured their flesh. Still another broke and mangled their bones. Finally, a black rain fell day and night.

The few who escaped into the trees became monkeys, "which is why monkeys look like men."

There was no light, no sun, no moon, no stars.

"I shall be the sun," one of the gods had said. He had been pleased with himself. "Great is my splendor!" he had shouted across the heavens. "My eyes are silver, resplendent as precious stones, like emeralds. My teeth shine like precious stones, like the face of heaven. My nose shines far like the moon, my throat is silver, and the face of the earth is lit up when it passes before my throne. In short, I am the Sun, I am the Moon."

But he was a great boaster; his light had reached only to the distant horizon. And it had been impossible even to see the face of the sun, the moon, or the stars.

This had happened at the time the deluge had destroyed the men of wood. The sun god himself had perished after two other gods had robbed him of his riches. In the fight, one had had an arm torn off.

The earth remained without light or any human beings. The gods tried once more. They finally created a new man out of yellow and white corn. This seed was brought to the gods by Yac, the Wildcat; by Utué, the Coyote; by Qul, the Parakeet; and by Hoh, the Crow.

The corn was ground, and "only ground corn was used to make the flesh of our fathers," according to Mayan legend. Four men were made simultaneously by Tepeu and Gucumatz.

"Since they looked like men, men they were . . . They spoke, conversed, saw and heard, walked, took hold of things. They were good and handsome men . . . They were given intelligence, and came to know everything there was in the world. They could see the forests, the rocks, the lakes, the seas, the mountains, and the valleys. Truly, they were admirable men."

Four beautiful wives were created, and the tribes soon multiplied to "a great number of black men and white men, and men of many classes and many tongues."

The four men became the rulers of the tribes. They led the Quichés to settle all the land, to build and to conquer, they and their children after them. But there was one who never had any children.

At last the sun came into being, and at the first dawn, the people waited for it to appear on the top of the highest mountain. The *quetzal* sang, and in that first glorious dawn over the earth, the people discovered god and all the richness and beauty of the earth.

The people asked their god Toquel to give them fire. "We are dying of cold," they pleaded.

It was given to them, but a great deluge extinguished it. "We are dying of cold," the people wailed.

"Don't worry," Toquel told them, and he promptly produced fire out of his shoe.

Neighboring tribes were still without fire, and they came to beg for it. This was denied. The great leader, Xilbalba, who flew on bat wings, told those without fire to go back again and just how to ask for it.

"Have mercy on us!" they cried, chattering with cold.

"What will you give us for our mercy?"

"Well, we can give you money."

"Money, we don't want."

"What do you want?"

"We shall ask Toquel and let you know."

They asked Toquel, and he said, "Let them give you their breasts and armholes for sacrifice. I want their hearts to hold in my arms. If they don't wish to do this, don't give them fire."

The emissaries agreed to provide victims for sacrifice. At once, they were given fire and quickly warmed their freezing bodies. But the god of one tribe flew through the smoke disguised as a bat and stole the fire. It was some time before everybody had fire.

Popol Vuh gives the Mayas' prayers to Huracán after they had conquered Soccotayá:

"Oh Thou, beautiful as the day! Thou, Huracán, Heart of Heaven, Heart of Earth, Thou gave us rivers, gave us sons and daughters. Bring us here also Thy glory and Thy riches; Grant Life and Growth to our sons and vassals. Let them multiply and grow, those who feed and sustain themselves; those

who invoke Thee on the roads, in the fields, on the banks of
the river, in the ravines, under the trees, under the vines . . .
Let their existence be good, those who give Thee Thy substance, and put food in Thy mouth, in the presence of Thee,
Heart of Heaven, Heart of the Earth, clothed in majesty. . . ."

Bibliography

The chief sources utilized by the author are in Spanish, but there have been numbers of authentic and exciting books written in English. A partial list follows.

Gann, Thomas. *Mystery Cities*. Scribner's, 1925.

Halle, Louis J., Jr. *River of Ruins*. Henry Holt, 1941.

Hewitt, Edgar L. *Ancient Life in Mexico and Central America*. Tudor, 1943.

Jessup, Marie Hendrick, and Simpson, Lesley Byrd. *Tales from Guatemala*. Scribner's, 1936.

Jones, C. L. *Guatemala, Past and Present*. University of Minnesota, 1940.

Joyce, Thomas Athol. *Maya and Mexican Art*. The Studio, London, 1927.

Kelsey, Vera, and Osborne, L. J. *Four Keys to Guatemala*. Funk & Wagnalls, 1948.

La Farge, Oliver L. *Santa Eulalia*. University of Chicago, 1947.

Morley, Sylvanius G. *The Ancient Mayas*. Stanford University, 1947.

Morley, Sylvanius G. *The Inscriptions at Copan.* Carnegie Institute, 1920.

Oglesby, Catherine. *Modern Primitive Arts of Mexico, Guatemala and the Southwest.* Whittlesey House, 1939.

Plenn, Virginia and Jaime. *A Guide to Modern Mexican Murals.* Tolteca, Mexico, 1963.

Redfield, Robert. *The Folk Culture of Yucatan.* University of Chicago, 1941.

Rodman, Selden. *Mexican Journal.* Devin-Adair, 1958.

Spinden, Herbert J. *Ancient Civilizations of Mexico and Central America.* American Museum of Natural History, 1922.

Stephens, John L. *Incidents of Travel in Central America, Chiapas and Yucatan.* 2 vols. Harper, 1841. New edition, edited by Richard L. Predmore, Rutgers University, 1956.

Stephens, John L. *Incidents of Travel in Yucatan.* Harper, 1843. New edition, edited by Victor W. Von Hagen, University of Oklahoma, 1962. Original edition reprinted by Dover (paperback) and John Smith.

Thompson, J. Eric. *The Civilization of the Mayas.* University of Chicago, 1936. Sixth Edition, Oceana, 1958.

Willard, T. A. *The City of the Sacred Well.* Century, 1921.

Index

153